When you move
a look moves inside me
and eats there what I eat.

— **Gregory Kan**

E Koro – kaua e haere
Don't leave
who will growl
when we're out of tune
so that music flows
from broken guitar strings

— **Haare Williams**

You don't have to have the baby right now
you just have to decide whether someday
you will.

— **Ashleigh Young**

We had a horse. And that,
for us, mattered more than a house.
You can't ride a house
out of town.

— **Sam Hunt**

I pull into the station,
tell them where I'm headed,
ask which has fewer calories,
diesel or unleaded.

— **Erik Kennedy**

The space between Earth and Mars
is the space between two worlds.
It is the space between two words.

— **Tim Upperton**

I gave to you a rock
from which you built a wall
then you stood there at the top
making me feel small

— **Jacq Carter**

Somewhere a poet
is cleaning a bathroom.
Somewhere a cleaner
is writing a poem.

— **Rachel McAlpine**

Remember Me

RE MEM BER ME

Poems to Learn by Heart from Aotearoa New Zealand

Edited by Anne Kennedy

With Robert Sullivan, consulting editor te reo Māori

AUCKLAND UNIVERSITY PRESS

First published 2023
Auckland University Press
University of Auckland
Private Bag 92019
Auckland 1142
New Zealand
www.aucklanduniversitypress.co.nz

© Anne Kennedy, and individual authors as credited, 2023

ISBN 978 1 86940 956 2

Published with the assistance of Creative New Zealand

A catalogue record for this book is available from the National Library of New Zealand

This book is copyright. Apart from fair dealing for the purpose of private study, research, criticism or review, as permitted under the Copyright Act, no part may be reproduced by any process without prior permission of the publisher. The moral rights of the authors have been asserted.

Book and cover design by Floor van Lierop
(thisisthem.com)

Printed in China through Asia Pacific Offset Group Ltd
This book was printed on FSC® certified paper

Contents

1   Introduction: Love the Poems

THE POEMS

Whakataukī / Wisdom

8   James K. Baxter —— HIGH COUNTRY WEATHER

9   James K. Baxter —— *From* JERUSALEM SONNETS (1)

10   Airini Beautrais —— CHARM FOR THE WINTER SOLSTICE

10   Airini Beautrais —— CHARM TO GET SAFELY HOME

11   Arapera Hineira Blank —— DREAMTIME

13   Jenny Bornholdt —— INSTRUCTIONS FOR HOW TO GET AHEAD OF YOURSELF WHILE THE LIGHT STILL SHINES

14   Jenny Bornholdt —— THE OX CLIMBED A FIR TREE

15   Sarah Broom —— HOLDING THE LINE

16   Cadence Chung —— CONFESSION BOX

17   Glenn Colquhoun —— AN ATTEMPT TO PREVENT THE DEATH OF AN OLD WOMAN

19   Mary Cresswell —— EVENSONG

20   Allen Curnow —— WILD IRON

21   Rangi Faith —— UNFINISHED CROSSWORD

22   Bernadette Hall —— REALLY & TRULY

23   Mohamed Hassan —— THE GUEST HOUSE

25   Dinah Hawken —— FAITH

26   Andrew Johnston —— HOW TO FLY

27   Rachel McAlpine —— LETTING GO

28   Cilla McQueen —— HOMING IN

29   Bill Manhire —— LITTLE PRAYERS

30   Te Kumeroa Ngoingoi Pēwhairangi —— KAUA RĀ HEI HURI NOA / DO NOT TURN AWAY

32   Kiri Piahana-Wong —— THIS IS IT

34	essa may ranapiri —— HAVE YOU GONE OUT AT NIGHT IN YOUR FAVOURITE DRESS AND THEN FELT LIKE SHIT?
35	Helen Rickerby —— WOOD / SPRING
36	Keri-Anne Stephens —— WAI ORA
38	Robert Sullivan —— KARAKIA WHAKAKAPI
40	J. C. Sturm —— UNTITLED
40	J. C. Sturm —— LET GO, UNLEARN, GIVE BACK
41	Apirana Taylor —— HAKA
42	Tayi Tibble —— A KARAKIA 4 A HUMBLE SKUX
45	Anthony Tipene-Matua —— HEI WHAKAWĀTEA I TE ARA
46	Brian Turner —— SKY
47	Arielle Walker —— KAWAKAWA
48	Sue Wootton —— WHAT CAN'T BE FORGIVEN

Odes

50	Tusiata Avia —— MY DOG
51	Tusiata Avia —— ODE TO DA LIFE
52	Ursula Bethell —— *From* AT THE LIGHTING OF THE LAMPS (VI)
53	Jenny Bornholdt —— IN THE GARDEN
54	Geoff Cochrane —— CONSOLATION PRIZE
55	Eileen Duggan —— THE SONG OF THE KINGFISHER
56	Sia Figiel —— *From* SONGS OF THE FAT BROWN WOMAN
58	Paula Green —— AFTER MODERNISM
59	Dinah Hawken —— PURE SCIENCE
61	Nicole Titihuia Hawkins —— AHO
62	Keri Hulme —— THE BOND OF BEES
63	Keri Hulme —— WINESONG 27
64	Sam Hunt —— *From* FOUR BOW-WOW POEMS (3)
65	Kevin Ireland —— A NEW TUNE
66	Erik Kennedy —— THERE'S NO PLACE LIKE THE INTERNET IN SPRINGTIME
67	Michele Leggott —— WHAT IS
68	Anna Livesey —— AUTUMN DAY
69	Bill Manhire —— HUIA
70	Bill Manhire —— KEVIN
71	Gregory O'Brien —— SONG
72	Bob Orr —— SONG TO CHELSEA WHARF

73	Vincent O'Sullivan —— THE SENTIMENT OF GOODLY THINGS
74	essa may ranapiri —— SILENCE, PART 2
76	Michael Steven —— AFTER TRAKL
77	Hone Tuwhare —— HAIKU (1)
78	Hone Tuwhare —— RAIN / UA
80	Hone Tuwhare —— SUN O (2)
81	Oscar Upperton —— CHILD'S FIRST DICTIONARY
82	Richard von Sturmer —— BASO IS UNWELL
82	Richard von Sturmer —— *From* SPARROW NOTEBOOK
83	Bryan Walpert —— SONG
85	Ian Wedde —— ABAT-JOUR
85	Ian Wedde —— *From* SHADOW STANDS UP (6), (18)
87	Briar Wood —— PADDLE CRAB

Whenua, Moana, Rangi / Earth, Sea, Sky

90	James K. Baxter —— BLOW, WIND OF FRUITFULNESS
91	Ursula Bethell —— DETAIL
91	Ursula Bethell —— TIME
92	Ben Brown —— PŪRIRI
93	Alistair Te Ariki Campbell —— THE RETURN
94	Geoff Cochrane —— OUR CITY AND ITS HILLS
95	Geoff Cochrane —— THE SEA THE LANDSMAN KNOWS
96	Ruth Dallas —— MILKING BEFORE DAWN
97	Eileen Duggan —— THE TIDES RUN UP THE WAIRAU
98	David Eggleton —— EDGELAND
99	Rangi Faith —— KARAKIA TO A SILENT ISLAND
100	Rangi Faith —— SPRING STAR
101	Denis Glover —— HOME THOUGHTS
101	Denis Glover —— THRENODY
102	Denis Glover —— THE MAGPIES
103	Dinah Hawken —— DRAMA
104	Jeffrey Paparoa Holman —— *From* THE LATE GREAT BLACKBALL BRIDGE SONNETS (XXIII)
105	Keri Hulme —— THE WINE-RICH ARTERIES
106	Robin Hyde —— THE LAST ONES
107	Cilla McQueen —— OUT THE BLACK WINDOW
108	Karlo Mila —— MANUHIRI

109 John Newton —— BEETLE
110 Bob Orr —— SONG TO RANGITOTO
112 Kiri Piahana-Wong —— AFTER THE SUN
113 Elizabeth Smither —— HERE COME THE CLOUDS
114 Brian Turner —— *From* FACES IN THE WATER
116 Hone Tuwhare —— RAIN REIGN / ŪA UAUA
118 Briar Wood —— PAEWAI O TE MOANA

Love Songs

120 Fleur Adcock —— COMMENT
121 Te Awhina Rangimarie Arahanga —— POHUTUKAWA PLAYS
THE BLUES
122 Nick Ascroft —— CORPSE SEEKS SIMILAR
124 Hinemoana Baker —— MATARIKI, E
125 Serie Barford —— A MATTER OF TIME
126 Ursula Bethell —— COMPENSATION
127 Hera Lindsay Bird —— I HAVE COME BACK FROM THE DEAD TO
TELL YOU THAT I LOVE YOU
128 Peter Bland —— THE CABIN
129 Behrouz Boochani —— FORGIVE ME MY LOVE
131 Jenny Bornholdt —— WEDDING SONG
133 Bub Bridger —— WILD DAISIES
134 Robbie Burns —— TO MARY IN HEAVEN / KI A MERI I TE RANGI
137 Alistair Te Ariki Campbell —— ROOTS
138 Jacq Carter —— E NOHO RĀ
140 Glenn Colquhoun —— A SPELL REFUSING TO CONSIDER THE
MENDING OF A BROKEN HEART
141 Ruth Dallas —— A GIRL'S SONG
142 Eileen Duggan —— THE BUSHFELLER
143 Bernadette Hall —— LIVING OUT HERE ON THE PLAINS
144 Nicole Titihuia Hawkins —— HE PIKO
145 Sam Hunt —— PORIRUA FRIDAY NIGHT
146 Kevin Ireland —— EACH DAY WOULD END
148 Anna Jackson —— THE TREEHOUSE
149 Gregory Kan —— [WHEN YOU MOVE]
150 Michele Leggott —— WILD LIGHT
151 Jiaqiao Liu —— TO A FUTURE YOU (I)

152 Jiaqiao Liu —— THAT HAND IS FOR HOLDING
153 Gregory O'Brien —— A PATRIOT OF THE TIME OF DAY
154 Gregory O'Brien —— A VISITING CARD
155 Joanna Margaret Paul —— THE DILETTANTE
156 Ruby Solly —— HOW TO MEET YOUR FUTURE HUSBAND IN
    HIS NATURAL HABITAT
157 Robert Sullivan —— AROHANUI
158 Paraire Hēnare Tomoana —— PŌKAREKARE ANA / THE WATERS
    OF WAIAPU
160 Hone Tuwhare —— NOCTURNE / ORIORI O TE PŌ
162 Albert Wendt —— IN YOUR ENIGMA
163 Sue Wootton —— MAGNETIC SOUTH
164 Ngati Whakahemo —— HE WAIATA AROHA / A SONG OF LOVE

Whānau

168 Fleur Adcock —— FOR A FIVE-YEAR-OLD
169 Tusiata Avia —— HELICOPTER
170 James K. Baxter —— CHARM FOR HILARY
171 Alistair Te Ariki Campbell —— FRIEND
172 Janet Charman —— THE PRESENT TABLE
173 Glenn Colquhoun —— A SPELL TO BE USED WHEN ADDRESSING
    THE BIRTH OF A CHILD
174 Sam Hunt —— MY FATHER SCYTHING
175 Sam Hunt —— MY FATHER TODAY
176 Anna Jackson —— CATULLUS FOR BABIES
177 Anna Jackson —— JOHNNY'S MINUTE
178 Cilla McQueen —— JOANNA
179 Fardowsa Mohamed —— TUESDAY
180 Gregory O'Brien —— THE LOCATION OF THE LEAST PERSON
181 Roma Potiki —— BIG SUSANAH
182 Jessie Puru —— WHĀNGAI
183 Robert Sullivan —— VOICE CARRIED MY FAMILY, THEIR NAMES
    AND STORIES
184 Albert Wendt —— SON
185 Haare Williams —— KOROUA
187 Ashleigh Young —— TRIOLET WITH BABY

Histories, Stories

190 Johanna Aitchison —— MISS DUST LOSES HER KEY
191 James K. Baxter —— LAMENT FOR BARNEY FLANAGAN
193 Ben Brown —— THE BROTHER COME HOME
195 Ben Brown —— TRUE HORI STORY
196 Janet Charman —— *From* HIGH DAYS AND HOLY DAYS (8)
197 Allen Curnow —— HOUSE AND LAND
199 Allen Curnow —— THE SKELETON OF THE GREAT MOA IN THE
CANTERBURY MUSEUM, CHRISTCHURCH
200 Ruth Dallas —— TINKER, TAILOR
201 Murray Edmond —— MR WAT
202 Fiona Farrell —— CHARLOTTE O'NEIL'S SONG
203 Bernadette Hall —— EARLY SETTLER
204 Sam Hunt —— WE HAD A HORSE
205 Andrew Johnston —— HYPERMARKET
206 Erik Kennedy —— THE CLASS ANXIETY COUNTRY SONG
207 Bill Manhire —— AN INSPECTOR CALLS
208 Ria Masae —— PAROUSIA
210 Tuini Ngāwai —— NGĀ RONGO / THE NEWS
212 Janet Newman —— THE SHEARER
213 Nina Mingya Powles —— LAST ECLIPSE
214 Jessie Puru —— MATARIKI
215 Elizabeth Smither —— MIRIAM'S WEDDING DRESS
216 Robert Sullivan —— WAKA 99
218 Apirana Taylor —— POEM FOR A PRINCESS
219 Chris Tse —— [ON SUNDAY]
220 Tim Upperton —— SPACE
221 Richard von Sturmer —— MONDAY 26 JUNE
222 David M'Kee Wright —— SHEARING'S COMING

Politics

224 Hana Pera Aoake —— *From* PERHAPS WE SHOULD HAVE STAYED
225 Behrouz Boochani —— THE BLACK KITE
226 Jacq Carter —— AROHA
228 Janet Charman —— THE LECTURE ON JUDY GRAHN
229 David Eggleton —— MY INNER AOTEAROA

230	David Eggleton —— PICTURES OF HOME
231	David Eggleton —— PRIME TIME
232	A. R. D. Fairburn —— IN THE YOUNGER LAND
233	Fiona Farrell —— THE THREAD
234	Gregory Kan —— [THERE'S A ROOM]
235	Anne Kennedy —— I WAS A FEMINIST IN THE EIGHTIES
237	Anne Kennedy —— THESE SCHOLARS AT THE PICNIC ONE DAY
239	Rachel McAlpine —— *From* SOMEWHERE A CLEANER (7)
240	Cilla McQueen —— TIMEPIECE
241	Selina Tusitala Marsh —— CALABASH BREAKERS
242	Courtney Sina Meredith —— BROWN GIRLS IN BRIGHT RED LIPSTICK
244	J. C. Sturm —— HE WAIATA TENEI MO PARIHAKA
246	Robert Sullivan —— OLD GOVERNMENT HOUSE
247	Leilani Tamu —— HOW TO MAKE A COLONIAL CAKE
249	Apirana Taylor —— SAD JOKE ON A MARAE
250	Chris Tse —— SUPER MODEL MINORITY — REINCARNATIONS
251	Hone Tuwhare —— NO ORDINARY SUN

HOW TO MEMORISE AND RECITE A POEM

254	Zech Soakai: Verse, Vessel and Voice
258	Rosalind Ali: On Teaching, Learning and Performing Poetry
262	Contributors and Sources
273	Thanks

Introduction: Love the Poems

*I learnt to love the songs which my people sang to
suit any and every occasion of their social life.*

— NGĀ MŌTEATEA: THE SONGS, PART ONE[1]

*When I began to listen to poetry, it's when I began to
listen to the stones, and I began to listen to what the
clouds had to say, and I began to listen to others.*

— JOY HARJO, US POET LAUREATE[2]

To remember a poem is to carry it with you always – the poem a distillation of thought, feeling, sound. To remember a poem is to go freely, without your keys, your bag, your baggage, yet to possess a valuable taonga. It's the ability to speak a poem out loud, to yourself, to the air, to your folks. There's a reason we say 'off by heart' when we commit words to memory: to remember a poem is to hold that poem close to your heart.

This book brings together a wide range of poems, all written by Aotearoa poets, which lend themselves to being memorised and recited. It suggests ways to read, learn and perform poetry, both historical and contemporary, for our times.

Poetry has its roots in the spoken – chants, rhymes, narratives – and even after hundreds of years of printing, it's remarkable that the thrill of poetry performance is as vital as ever. Over the last quarter century, oral poetry has had a huge resurgence globally via the internet and through the rise of literary festivals, poetry readings and poetry slams. Nowadays, the practice of performing poems live is universal. *Remember Me* presents poems that have been previously published on the page – this is not a Spoken Word anthology, although it is undoubtedly inspired by the slam phenomenon that made poetry aural again. What seems certain: the reach and impact of recited poetry is enormous.

Remember Me is not the first anthology of its kind. Among several such volumes in English, there have been *By Heart: 101 Poems to Remember*, edited by Ted Hughes,[3] and *Poetry by Heart: A Treasury of Poems to Read Aloud*, introduced by Andrew Motion.[4] These works have focused on the English and American canons; not a single Pacific poem appears. *Remember Me* is the first anthology of Aotearoa poems chosen specifically to memorise and recite.

The oral tradition is clearly important to Aotearoa, from haka and waiata, to sea shanties and ballads, to the rhythms of Ruth Dallas, the list poems of Selina Tusitala Marsh, the vernacular of Sam Hunt, the distillations of Bill Manhire, the immigrant testimonies of Mohamed Hassan, the bilingual lyric poems of Jacq Carter, the Buddhist-inspired tanka of Richard von Sturmer – and many more. The poems chosen here employ a kind of music to convey perception and image, occasion and story, and often the big emotions of love and loss. Overall, works that highlight memory and performance seem like a good way to explore and display Aotearoa's poetic treasures.

My interest in putting together this anthology goes way back and is personal. First was seeing how easily my children could learn a poem. Inspired by Ian McEwan's novel *Saturday*,[5] in which the protagonist pays his grandchildren to learn poems off by heart, I offered my children five dollars for every poem they could memorise. This continued until I couldn't afford it any more. The important thing is that my now-grown children still know these poems, and young people's brains are sponge-like. My own early brush with New Zealand poetry was as a thirteen-year-old at school reading Sam Hunt's 'Porirua Friday Night' and being astounded that a poem could sound like us. It tripped off the tongue, stayed in my head, and it felt marvellous to be able to recite this fun but poignant poem. I also recall my dad reciting screeds of *The Rime of the Ancient Mariner*[6] which he'd learned at school and, by association, *I* know: 'The fair breeze blew, the white foam flew, / The furrow followed free; / We were the first that ever burst / Into that silent sea.' My mum dispensed bits of Shakespeare and the Bible in equal measure. Learned poems have good traction; they go down the generations.

In later years, as a teacher of writing, I noticed that when I asked my students to learn a poem by heart, it enhanced not just their enjoyment and engagement with the poem, but their confidence in approaching other poems. Reciting a poem brings together so much of ourselves: our intellect, memory, emotions, ear, voice, and our communication with others.

A poem learned *by heart* can, reputedly, ease that little pumping organ, the heart. In *Stressed, Unstressed: Classic Poems to Ease the Mind*, it is suggested that 'a poem committed to memory can often serve as a kind of mantra in times of stress'.[7] Sound, idea, beauty, music, all help us get by. But if a remembered poem is soothing, it can also be challenging, entertaining, instructional, observational. Poems represent all that we are.

The poems here have been chosen with the idea of reciting them in different ways, in different places – maybe to a poetry night audience, to your whānau or flatmates, to yourself or simply in your own head. Some poems will lend themselves to occasions such as weddings, funerals and public holidays, but most are everyday words.

To organise the poems, I became a sheepdog – although poems are like cats, and in the end seven broad categories seemed to find their place in the sun. What makes a poem read-out-loudable or simply memorable is a tougher question. It seems to be to do with sound and communication – how a poem *re*sounds for the performer, how it appeals to the listener.

The selected poems tend to have one or more of the following elements: **rhythm** (overall tempo and pace, as in Hone Tuwhare's 'Rain' and Jenny Bornholdt's 'The ox climbed a fir tree'), **metre** (stresses, as in Eileen Duggan's 'The Tides Run up the Wairau' and Kevin Ireland's 'A New Tune'), **rhyme** (as in James K. Baxter's

'Blow, wind of fruitfulness' and Bill Manhire's 'An Inspector Calls'), **repetition** (as in Glenn Colquhoun's 'An attempt to prevent the death of an old woman' and Sia Figiel's 'Songs of the fat brown woman'), **narrative** (as in Denis Glover's 'The Magpies' and Cilla McQueen's 'Timepiece'), **declamatory style** (as in J. C. Sturm's 'Let go, unlearn, give back' and Apirana Taylor's 'Sad Joke on a Marae'), and/or **humour** (as in Tusiata Avia's 'Helicopter' and Tayi Tibble's 'A Karakia 4 a Humble Skux').

Some poems are short and pithy (such as Alan Curnow's 'Wild Iron' and J. C. Sturm's 'Untitled'), but brevity is not a prerequisite for learning a poem. The poems include a range of difficulty in terms of learning off by heart, with some poems relatively simple while others are a challenge. It's worth noting that committing a poem to memory isn't easy. It takes time and effort, but the rewards pay off.

To help readers, Rosalind Ali (influential high school teacher of English literature and creative writing) and Zech Soakai (acclaimed poet and high school teacher of English literature) offer, from their first-hand experience working with young people and poetry, ways to memorise and perform poetry. These recommendations are for everyone.

One of the most interesting aspects about how a recited poem works is the issue of the poet, the speaker. How does 'I' work coming out of someone else's mouth? 'I' can be universal, as in Geoff Cochrane's 'Consolation Prize'. What doesn't tend to translate to recitation are poems that are autobiographical, that assume a persona. The same is true for poems where the visual arrangement is paramount. That means that not every Aotearoa poet is in this book, including many of my favourite poets.

In the end, what lends a poem to being recited is what makes a poem fly in the first place: whatever works. So this book has famous poems, little-known poems, long poems, short poems. Each poem will mean something different to each person.

When we learn a poem off by heart, we embody it. It is stored in our brain, on our tongue, in our ear. It stays with us. American poet Robert Pinsky writes in *The Sounds of Poetry: A Brief Guide* –

'Poetry is among other things a technology for remembering.'[8] I hope the poems collected here are memorable, lovable and will be cherished. I hope readers (listeners, speakers) will enjoy this book and also go beyond it and find many other poems to remember.

Ngā mihi,
Anne Kennedy
Tāmaki Makaurau, 2023

References

1 Ngata, Apirana (ed.), *Ngā Mōteatea: The Songs, Part One*, translated by Pei Te Hurinui Jones (Auckland University Press, 2004, pp. xxxvi).

2 Harjo, Joy, 'Joy Harjo Reflects on the "Spirit of Poetry"', interview with Jim Lehrer (PBS, www.pbs.org/newshour/show/joy-harjo-reflects-on-the-spirit-of-poetry).

3 Hughes, Ted (ed.), *By Heart: 101 Poems to Remember* (Faber & Faber, 2002).

4 Motion, Andrew (ed.), *Poetry by Heart: A Treasury of Poems to Read Aloud* (Penguin, 2014).

5 McEwan, Ian, *Saturday* (Jonathan Cape, 2005).

6 Coleridge, Samuel Taylor, *The Rime of the Ancient Mariner* (Poetry Foundation, 2022, www.poetryfoundation.org/poems/43997/the-rime-of-the-ancient-mariner-text-of-1834).

7 Bate, Jonathan and Paula Byrne (eds), *Stressed, Unstressed: Classic Poems to Ease the Mind* (William Collins, 2016, p. 11).

8 Pinsky, Robert (ed.), *The Sounds of Poetry: A Brief Guide* (Farrar Straus and Giroux, 1999).

The Poems

Whakataukī / wisdom

James K. Baxter

High Country Weather

Alone we are born
  And die alone;
Yet see the red-gold cirrus
  Over snow-mountain shine.

Upon the upland road
  Ride easy, stranger:
Surrender to the sky
  Your heart of anger.

From Jerusalem Sonnets

1.

The small grey cloudy louse that nests in my beard
Is not, as some have called it, 'a pearl of God' –

No, it is a fiery tormentor
Waking me at two a.m.

Or thereabouts, when the lights are still on
In the houses in the pa, to go across thick grass

Wet with rain, feet cold, to kneel
For an hour or two in front of the red flickering

Tabernacle light – what He sees inside
My meandering mind I can only guess –

A madman, a nobody, a raconteur
Whom He can joke with – 'Lord,' I ask Him,

'Do You or don't You expect me to put up with lice?'
His silent laugh still shakes the hills at dawn.

Airini Beautrais

Charm for the Winter Solstice

A feather   a leaf
a stone   a bone
a dead
      town
         road.

Incandescent
snow on the hills.
The forest dark below.

Charm to Get Safely Home

It is a wet night but I am dry.
It is a dark night but the way is light.
The last cries of birds chip the air
the scent of new logs trucks past.
I could keep walking far beyond
where I am going.

Arapera Hineira Blank

(Ngāti Porou, Ngāti Kahungunu, Rongowhakaata,
Te Aitanga a Māhaki)

Dreamtime

When you feel
heaviness of spirit
belly tighten
deep hurt under your heart,
reach out for someone,
no one comes,
turn inwards.

Fall into gentle breathing,
listen to the music
of silence,
lie still, float, on
velvet black,
till your body
is bathed in calm,
slowly unfold your
pain-easing dream.

Imagine you came
into this world
in a cloud of
red-orange-gossamer
silk, shimmering up
with the dawn, along,
down to a dew-damp earth,
that warmed with you,
filled her people

song-rich with hope
for spiritual peace,
now,
tomorrow, and tomorrow.

'The sun rises,
the sun sets,
the sun rises.

He rā ka whiti
he rā ka tō
he rā ka whiti.'

Jenny Bornholdt

Instructions for how to get ahead of yourself while the light still shines

If you have a bike, get on it at night
and go to the top of the Brooklyn Hill.

When you reach the top
start smiling — this is Happy Valley Road.

Pedal at first, then let the road take you down
into the dark as black as underground
broken by circles of yellow lowered by the street lights.

As you come to each light
you will notice a figure
racing up behind.
Don't be scared
this is you creeping up on yourself.
As you pass under the light
you will sail past yourself into the night.

The ox climbed a fir tree
From Estonian Songs

The ox climbed a fir tree
to see what he could see.

He cried ah, my love
this view from above
is quite splendid,
you are smaller
than a dove.

He cried
ah, my love
I am enthralled
but now I can't see you
at all.

Sarah Broom

holding the line

when I feel feverish
I take the full moon
and place it on my brow
like a flannel

it is so cool because it has just
been swimming in the sea

when I feel that my heart
is clapping out of time
I take it out and throw it
up among the stars

who know all there is to know
about holding the line

Cadence Chung

confession box

i made my cousin afraid of spiders last holidays
lord forgive me he used to pick them up between
his fingers and carry them outside like a benevolent
unblemished giant but we said ewww and yuck so
many times that he thought it was wrong
lord forgive me i wasn't hungry for dinner because
i ate all the grapes that we had been saving for
Saturday so cold and so ripe forgive me i told my
friend i was over my fear of spiders but i still
hairsprayed one to death the other night until
it became tacky and its legs slowed to a stop
i'm sorry i dissected a bug and painted its wings
and kept them for myself when i meant to
give them to a friend lord i'm sorry for talking
behind my classmate's back about the pointlessness
of her colour-coded notes and lord i know that
these are perhaps not sins but i think
sins are little things like telling children
the dead bugs on the road are just sleeping

Glenn Colquhoun

An attempt to prevent the death of an old woman

Old woman, don't go, don't
go outside into dark weather
Out into the night's wet throat
There is cooking on your stove
Old woman, don't go.

Don't go old woman, don't go
Down beneath that deep sea
Down onto its soft bed
There are still fish to be caught
Old woman, don't go.

Don't go old woman, don't go
Up into that cold sky
Hung against those sharp stars
The light is still on in your room
Old woman, don't go.

Don't go old woman, don't go
Bent into that slippery wind
Listening for its clean voice
There are songs still left to sing
Old woman, don't go.

Don't go old woman, don't go
Walking beside that steep cliff
Watching where the sea flowers
There are daisies on your lawn
Old woman, don't go.

Don't go old woman, don't go
Lifting in those strange arms
Caught against that dark chest
There are people left to hold
Don't go, old woman, don't go.

Mary Cresswell

Evensong

I am the dirge
they sang in the dark
when the stars began to fall

I am the carol
that shot to the sky
while the children huddled the wall

I am the glass
the singer broke
from too many rooms away

I am the clock
whose penultimate stroke
has nearly finished the day

I am the beak
I am the tail

I am the teeth
I am the gale

I am the face
and I am the veil

while the stars begin to fall.

Allen Curnow

Wild Iron

Sea go dark, dark with wind,
Feet go heavy, heavy with sand,
Thoughts go wild, wild with the sound
Of iron on the old shed swinging, clanging:
Go dark, go heavy, go wild, go round,
    Dark with the wind,
    Heavy with the sand,
Wild with the iron that tears at the nail
And the foundering shriek of the gale.

Rangi Faith
(Kāi Tahu, Ngāti Kahungunu)

Unfinished Crossword

If they say:
you may find a friend
in the least likely of places,
I have, here –
fifteen across, ataahua, the beautiful one;
and here – six across – aperira,
the month of the leaf fall;

here – eleven down – aue!
and all the gods crying
in all the places
that ever were & still
      & still do;

and here – five down – atua,
the gods calling your god,
like the candle flame
and the star in the wide night –
a beckoning.

Bernadette Hall

Really & Truly

I took my anger
running on the beach.
She said, 'You've got to
put me on a longer leash, bitch.
How else can I dabble
my tootsies in the water
and roll in the stinking weed?'

I took my anger
walking round the park.
She said, 'You know
I've always been scared
of the dark
and now you've started
the fucking dogs barking.'

I took my anger
out for morning tea.
She sat there as good as gold,
smiling beside me.
'We don't know what you keep
going on about,' they all said to me.
'She's really lovely. Truly.'

Mohamed Hassan

The guest house
(for Al Noor and Linwood Mosques)

In this house
we have one rule:

*bring only what you want to
leave behind*

we open doors
with both hands
passing batons
from death to life

come share with us
this tiny peace

we built from broken tongues
and one-way boarding passes

from kauri bark
and scholarships

from kaitiaki
and kin

in this house
we are

all broken
all strange
all guests

we are holding
space for you

         stranger
         friend

Dinah Hawken

Faith

Here is a white mask.
You will need it to get around the city.

Here are your waders
and your fireproof vests.

While colour leaches from the world
you will well up with sorrow.

When coral fades and the sea rises
you will take life above the waterline

and extract from the tolerant earth
insane amounts of faith.

Think of saris lifting like wildfire.
And cows that were turned into gods.

Think silk, spice and sailing ship.
Enter a temple and pray for a temperate rain.

Andrew Johnston

How to Fly

Try anything, like the young birds
—it's late spring—in the rose garden

falling and—just in time—recalling
something they haven't had time to learn

and carrying on this conversation
consisting of the word 'Yes'. Their

mothers lift beetles from the blooms' silk nests,
clean the buds of aphids; the young

fall and flap and open their pink silk mouths for food
and say 'Yes'. And then they fly.

Rachel McAlpine

Letting go

Over and over again you've had to let go
and as you get old you have to do it
more often, more shocking and more.
You've done it before.

You let go of your favourite toy
when it lost its shine.
You let go of houses and friends
and, after all, that turned out fine.

You let your children fly the nest
you passed that test. But now
you must let go of beauty
and habits galore. You're losing score.

And yes, it's hard.
It breaks your heart.
Something is clinging and it is you
and you know what you have to do.

Cilla McQueen

Homing In

Here again.
Dark's falling. Stand
on the corner of the verandah
in the glass cold clear
night, looking out
to emerald & ruby harbour
lights:
          too sharp to stay
out long,
               enough just to
greet the bones lying
on the moon
& two fishing boats
homing in.

Bill Manhire

Little Prayers
15 March 2019

Let the closing line be the opening line
Let us open ourselves to grief and shame
Let pain be felt and be felt again
May our eyes see when they cease crying
Let the closing line be the opening line

Let the seas storm, let the hills quake
Let us inspect what makes us ache
Let there be tasks we undertake
Let us make what we can make
When the seas storm and the hills shake

May the rivers and lakes and mountains shine
May every kiss be a coastline
May we sing once again for the first time
May the children be home by dinnertime
May the closing line be an opening line

Te Kumeroa Ngoingoi Pēwhairangi

(Te Whānau-ā-Ruataupare, Ngāti Porou)

Kaua rā hei huri noa

Kaua rā hei huri noa
Kaua hei whakahāwea
Mā ō mahi ka kitea koe
E te ao, e tō iwi Māori
Kua puāwai rawa ngā purapura
I ruia mai i ngā wā o tūā-whakarere
E toro nei ngā kāwai taura tangata
Hei hono i te aroha o ō tāua tīpuna
Te mana, te wehi
Awhitia ngā taonga kei memeha, kei ngaro
Kei tūkinotia e te ao
Puritia tō mana kei riro e!

Do not turn away

[Translated by Sir Timoti Kāretu and the Advisory Committee
for the Teaching of the Maori Language]

Do not turn away
Nor despise others
By your deeds will you be known
By society at large and by your own Maori people
The seeds sown since time immemorial
Are now in full bloom
And the human links are spread far and wide
Forging the love, the prestige, the respect of our ancestors
Give all your support to our cultural pursuits
Lest they become lifeless and die
Or be debased by the world at large
Retain your prestige, lest it be lost for all time!

Kiri Piahana-Wong
(Ngāti Ranginui, Chinese, English)

This is it

One day you're just
sitting there, doing something
that's not particularly
important, and the clouds
glacing the sky capture
your attention, and you
realise, with a start, that
this is it, this is
the shape of your life.

All these years waiting to
grow into something
fabulous, fitting, but
instead, just growing
bigger.

Not knowing what it
is that you want
anymore, or what
it isn't.

Too many things defined
by absences—the phone
that doesn't ring, the
empty fruit bowl. All
so mundane, not like
the absent lover you have
always dreamt of
having. Being possessed
by.

And now the starlight
pours down on your
face, millions of
light-years too late.
They're already dead.
But look. Look
how brightly
they shine.

essa may ranapiri

(Ngāti Raukawa, Te Arawa, Ngāti Pukeko, Clan Gunn)

Have you gone out at night in your favourite dress and then felt like shit?

got all my delusions
worked up about the party
the shed
the lap dance
the silver bowls
left in the garden the golden frogs on the lawn
someone wants to put fire on my stomach
i push my mouth onto small things
fingernails you clipped and left on the sill
fake lashes on the kitchen table
got all my delusions thinking that i won't become
    a statistic
because this gender is a death trap or something

Helen Rickerby

Wood / spring
From Ban Zhao

The wind itself is silent
It's only when it hits something
that it makes a sound
I was sure I heard a rushing waterfall
but when I looked, it was only a zephyr in the trees
The wind does not even know it is moving
until it meets an obstacle

If you stay in the same place
you are always moving backwards

Keri-Anne Stephens
(Ngāti Kahungunu)

Wai ora

Ka whakaarohia ngā pēhitanga o te wā
Kua mānakanaka,
Mānukanuka,
Mānatunatu
Kua ohooho te mauri
Kia mauri ohooho.

Ka kotahi atu au ki te Wai
Wai Māori
    Wai rere
        Wai ora
            Wairua
Ka māturuturu,
    Ka māringiringi
        Ka tāuhiuhi te uwhiuwhi

Ka hīrere te wai
Ka horoi te tinana
    Ka horoia te hinengaro
        Ka horohoroia te wairua

Kua tau te mauri
    Kua mauri tau
        Kua mahea
            Kua wātea
Kua whakanoa!
Kua ora ahau!

[Translation]

As I reflect upon the stresses of the time
I am apprehensive
Uncertain
Uneasy
I am restless
I am anxious.

I head into the Water
Pure water
    that flows
        and reinvigorates
            my spirit
It drizzles
Sprinkles down upon me
            Showers me

The water pours down upon me
It washes my body
    It clears my mind
        It purifies my soul

I am calmed
    I am settled
        My mind is cleared
            My wairua is unencumbered
I am cleansed!
I am alive!

Robert Sullivan
(Ngāpuhi, Kāi Tahu, Irish)

Karakia Whakakapi

I pā ahau ki a Papatūānuku
te whaea o te ao
ka tukua aku ringa ki Ranginui kei runga
te matua o te kikorangi
ā, papaki rawa iho te tau o taku ate
horomia iho i rō i te ngākau
ki te ipu wai roha
e pupuri ana i ngā tūmomo kōhatu:
te mea tūpono,
te āwangawanga,
te mokemoketanga,
te takinga,
kia kaha ai koe, roha ngā parirau
o te manawanui
ā, whakarērea nei te mihi
karangatia hī ki te whenua
karangatia hā ki te rangi
ka homai, ka hoatu ngā tāngata
mā roto i ēnei uaua
ōrite ki te rauiti uaua
o te raupua e mānu ana
ki roto i tērā ipu wai
ngā mihi ki a koe e te tuakana,
ngā mihi ki a koe e te tuahine,
me hōngi harirū tātou,
me pōrutu i ā tātou hoe
me whakahā rawa iho
me inu i te wai aroha
ka karanga tonu tātou i te whakamihi
ka tū i te hui nei kei runga i te whenua toitū
wirihia tonutia ngā ringa o te tira haukainga e.

[Translation]

I touch Papatūānuku my earthmother
    give hands up to Ranginui
my skyfather
    then beat both wings of the heart
skull it down through the pelvis
to a rosewater bowl
filling with stones: chance/angst/loneliness/failure
dip hands in this sprinkle
        heads in clarity pass the speech of
people on
blush and touch make love slowly (be careful)

we slide in a round of writhing
weeds that thrash a jive
expressed in a loud way (I'm out of my circle)
persevere beat your heart's wings
        fly out to greet them
shout 'Hii!' (hee) to the ground
shout 'Haa!' to the sky
through veins people give and take
    fine as those crossing a petal
    floating on a bowl
health to you brother (we hongi)
    health to you sister (we kiss)
splash your paddles
breathe deeply drink up
we've got a chant of unbroken
        tone/s to toast!
a meeting on respected grounds
an open sound so pure it shakes the host

J. C. Sturm
(Taranaki, Whakatōhea)

Untitled

The house is quiet now
And still.

No gale from the sea
No weeping in the garden
Or cry from the hill.

Later there will be
Stars and a moon
Tomorrow the sun.

Let go, unlearn, give back

Let go, relinquish
Charms, talismans, taonga.
Return them, in the turning time
To their source.

Unlearn, put aside
Chants, prayers, incantations.
Exchange them, in the changing time
For silence.

Give back, but gently
Loving and being loved.
Then leave them, in the leaving time

And go alone.

Apirana Taylor

(Ngāti Porou, Te Whānau-ā-Apanui, Ngāti Ruanui)

haka

when I hear the haka
i feel it in my bones
and in my wairua
the call of my tipuna
flashes like lightning
up and down my spine
it makes my eyes roll
and my tongue flick
it is the dance
of earth and sky
the rising sun
and the earth shaking
it is the first breath of life
eeeee aaa ha haaa

Tayi Tibble
(Te Whānau-ā-Apanui, Ngāti Porou)

A Karakia 4 a Humble Skux

I take a bath in my body of water
I take a bath in my body of water

I know I am the daughter of rangi papa tangaroa
I know I am the daughter of rangi papa tangaroa

& every yung god who fucked it up before me.
& every yung god who fucked it up before me.

Every day I breach the surface cleanly
Every day I breach the surface cleanly

& step out dripping so hard
& step out dripping so hard

ya better call a plumber.
ya better call a plumber.

God I'm a flex.
God I'm a flex.

I'm God's best sex.
I'm God's best sex.

I am made in the image of God.
I am made in the image of God.

I am made in the image of my mother.
I am made in the image of my mother.

I am made in the image of
I am made in the image of

my mountain
my river
my whenua.

my mountain
my river
my whenua.

Yeah I'm as fresh as my oldest tipuna.
Yeah I'm as fresh as my oldest tipuna.

Even when I'm lowkey I'm loud.
Even when I'm lowkey I'm loud.

Lil, but a million years old.
Lil, but a million years old.

I've been germinating like a seed
I've been germinating like a seed

been on my vibe like an atom
been on my vibe like an atom

& I am wilder than anything
& I am wilder than anything

my ancestors could have imagined.
my ancestors could have imagined.

So release the parts of me that call for change
So release the parts of me that call for change

but the energy is stale.
but the energy is stale.

I'm switching it all up
I'm switching it all up

fishing stars into the sea
fishing stars into the sea

and painting the skyful of whales.
and painting the skyful of whales.

Keep it humble, keep it skux.
Keep it humble, keep it skux.

Keep it pushing, keep it cute.
Keep it pushing, keep it cute.

I be in the marae doing the dishes
I be in the marae doing the dishes

cos there's mahi to do.
cos there's mahi to do.

Creator and Creation.
Creator and Creation.

I am made of the same
I am made of the same

star matter as legends.
star matter as legends.

Āmene.
Āmene.

Lesh go.
Lesh go.

Anthony Tipene-Matua

Hei whakawātea i te ara

Ākatia ki runga
Akuakuna ki raro
Rauiritia ki te ara tika
Kia wātea te ara takatū
Kia tū kaha, kia tū maia
Kia tū whakahī te wairua
Mai i te putanga i te pō
Ki te whaiao
Ki te ao mārama
Tihei
Mauri ora!

[Translation]

Cleanse above
Cleanse below
Clear the path ahead
To clear an open space
To stand with strength and resilience
To raise the spirit
As it emerges from the darkness
Into the daylight
Into the world of light.

Brian Turner

Sky

If the sky knew half
of what we're doing
down here

it would be stricken,
inconsolable,
and we would have

nothing but rain

Arielle Walker
(Taranaki, Ngāruahine, Ngāpuhi, Pākehā)

kawakawa

look first for the leaves with the most holes
(the hearts should be riddled with them, it means they are
healthy, it means that others have already eaten their fill
and left you with only the strongest pieces)

meld the oils into a salve
to soothe the sting of lost words
sliding from your stumbling tongue

the crushed leaves will dye a shade of soft olive green
that fades as fast as summer does
(better to drink it in and hold
the memory of colour instead)

Sue Wootton

What can't be forgiven

What can't be forgiven
must be lived with.
What can't be lived with
must be forgiven.
What can't be forgotten
must be knotted round your heart
softly as gossamer
hard as barbed wire.

Odes

Tusiata Avia

My dog

My dog name is Bingo.
All da dog name is Bingo.
Bingo is da bad dog.
He bite da Palagi mans on da foot.
Aunty Fale throw da big stone to Bingo
and make da sore on Bingo's leg.
Now Bingo walk on da 3 leg.

The Palagi mans he's stay at our house now
and everybody is very happy
specially Aunty who is showing to all da peoples
of our village how we have da Palagi.

Now Bingo no more sleep under da table
because Aunty say he's stink
and no good for da Palagi to smell da stink smell.

Bingo he sleep outside and eat da stone.
Only feed Bingo da stone everytime.
We call
BingoBingoBingo
and throw da stone to him
and laugh
HaHaHa
and da Palagi man shout to us
You kids stop throwing stones at the dog!

And Aunty Fale call us shit and pig
and chase us with da broom and hit us hardhard
on da leg and catch Pela by da hair and shake her
hardhard till Pela's hair is coming out
in Aunty's hand and Pela is cryingscreaming.

We call
BingoBingoBingo
and Bingo come runningrunning
and lick our sore
and grinning.

Ode to da life

You wan da Ode?
OK, I give you
Here my Ode to da life
Ia, da life is happy an perfek
Everybodys smile, everybodys laugh
Lot of food like Pisupo, Macdonal an Sapasui
Even da dog dey fat
You hear me, suga? Even da dog!

An all da Palagi dey very happy to us
Dey say Hey come over here to Niu Sila
Come an live wif us an eat da ice cream
An watch TV2 evry day
Days of Our Lives evry evry day
Hope an Beau an Roman an Tony De Mera.

Dat how I know my Ode to da life
An also Jesus – I not forget Jesus
He's say to us Now you can
Do anyfing you like
Have da boyfrien, drink da beer
Anyfing, even in front of your fadda
An never ever get da hiding
Jus happy an laughing evry time.

Ursula Bethell

From At the Lighting of the Lamps
(for Music)

vi.

Still the gold lights quiver
By hidden sea and river;

From the dim arena below
Shines their concerted glow;

And the bright stars answer still
Over above the hill.

The deep dome overhead
Is fully furnishéd

With lamps, and they are lit
To the outmost bounds of it.

And each mighty spark
Sheds its gentle light
Into the silent dark,
The silent night,
On and on, through the dark, the silent night.

Jenny Bornholdt

In the garden

In the garden
the bulbs run riot
root systems go
all over the place
we crack open huge dry
clods of earth and uncover
white bulbs of onion flowers
embedded like fossils
their roots like thin streamers
partying down through the soil.
So we have a white flower
propped on the top of a green stem
a plain enough thing
while underneath
the feelers are out
hooking into other systems
forming the network
the flower an undercover agent
posted on the watch
a decoy of simplicity.

Geoff Cochrane

Consolation Prize

I bring them home
on the bus, a
cluster of small
pink roses.

I shorten their
stalks with scissors
and put them in
a pickle jar.

They swell and fade;
each time I look
their petals seem
more numerous.

Eileen Duggan

The Song of the Kingfisher

Why do you sit, so dreamily, dreamily,
  Kingfisher over the stream,
Silent your beak, and silent the water,
  What is your dream?

A falling, a flashing of blue and silver,
  Child, he is deep in the stream,
Prey in his beak, and fear in the water—
  That was his dream!

Sia Figiel

From Songs of the fat brown woman
(for sista grace [nichols] and the fat black woman)

The fat brown woman move in the breeze
under the thatch of the small small fale
braiding sinnet
weaving stories
between the leaves of the pandanus

The fat brown woman sweat in the sun
lean on a coconut palm
swaying in the coconut sun
in colourful lavalava too small for her waist

The fat brown woman in the sea
is a sight to see
diving for blue fish red fish
an occasional eel
The fat brown woman walking home from the sea
is a sight to see

Around the fat brown woman there is
always a man or two
Big or small
Smiling smiling
At the way her hip sway
At the sound her thigh make
Around the fat brown woman there is
always a fly
or two
too

See the fat brown woman at a fa'alavelave
Directing the men the women
A fine mat here

A pig there
In her fat brown woman voice
in her fat brown woman style
gentle but firm
is the fat brown woman

When the fat brown woman hops on the bus the girls
and boys whisper
and men and women whisper
and children and cat whisper whisper
and pigs too sometimes
watch her sway
sway sway
and her arms moving like dat
and a shaking like dat
is her tummy too
they make room right behind the skinny
bus driver who gives her a big fat wink
the fat brown woman takes out a bright red
hanky wipes the sweat off her brow
pats her cheek
adjusts her dress/her bra/
her hip
chase away the flies
give the bus driver a mean look
Is going be a long way to market

So you can look all you want
And you can watch all you want
And you can stare all you want
But the fat brown woman will keep
swaying her hip
Keep swaying her hip
All the way to town

Paula Green

After Modernism

After Modernism I walked to the shops
to buy a loaf of bread and a bottle of milk
with the leaffrocked wind in my hair
and the waterlogged tyre in my ear
and the backblock road in my eye
and the woebegone fog in my nose
and the forgetmenot paper in my hand
and the slipknot word on my cheek
and the crosscrossed sign on my thigh
and the defrosted pronoun on my brow.

I saw a flowerpot that looked a lot like gorse
gorse that looked a lot like barleycorn
barleycorn that looked a lot like a harpsichord
a harpsichord that looked a lot like a hobbyhorse.

Dinah Hawken

Pure Science

If you are where you are
you see
where you are
and if you see where you are
you even know
who you are

which sounds ho-hum

but is scientific and scintillating
that is
being where you are

here

say in the garden
you see a green leaf
and you feel like a star

you *are* a star

and most likely shining

but others can't see
the shining
because they don't know
where *they* are

and you can't see the shining
because by wondering

whether you are shining
or not
and if so
how brightly

you've lost sight of
the leaf

Nicole Titihuia Hawkins
(Ngāti Kahungunu ki Te Wairoa, Ngāti Pāhauwera)

Aho

Hoki mai, hoki mai, hoki mai
e te tau, i tō ruku pō pō

ka puta mai tōu wairua
I raro i te tai kikorangi

kua tae mai koe mā raro kōpuka
nā te tote o ōu roimata

nuku mai ki te taha o te hahana
kia mahana ai ō toto pango

mauria mai ōu āwangawanga
ka whiua ki te puku o te ahi

titiro mai
mātakitaki ki te aru o te arero

e pūkana ana te mura
e whētero ana te mura

Haere, haere, haere ki runga
ki Ngā kurakura o Hinenuitepō.

Keri Hulme
(Kāi Tahu, Ngāti Māmoe, Nordic, Celtic)

The Bond of Bees

I'm blending my mind
with the ease of wine
from candle flowers
on a warm afternoon
and a bloom of bees
from the kamahi
resounds   resounds
in the quiet room

        spikes to the honey
        bees to the comb
        the yeast to the sweet mead
        and now the mead home

Winesong 27

All your passions
matched to mine
are as ebbtide matched to flood
are as water matched to blood
are vinegar to wine.

And yet
betimes surprised
by elusive shining fish
amongst the coral of your mind
I hesitate to break and wait
to find

all your passions
matched to mine
are as ebbtide matched to flood
are as water matched to blood
are vinegar to wine.

Sam Hunt

From Four Bow-Wow Poems

3.

Look, here are some simple facts:
You'll find in the poetry books
One thousand and twelve poems about cats

There are all sorts of poems about cats:
Cats chasing rats and cats wearing hats
And cats that simply sit on mats

But you look for bow-wow poetry
And it's quite a different story
Right now there are only three

And one more makes four . . .

They often ask me why
I write this bow-wow poetry

I'll tell you
And cross-my-heart it's true

I've got nothing else to do

Kevin Ireland

A New Tune

my harp is old
her strings are slack
her keys are locked
her paint is black

my hands have lost
their bold knack
but hear my sockets
knock and crack

Erik Kennedy

There's No Place Like the Internet in Springtime

There's no place like the internet in springtime!
Everything foals a new thing like itself,
and old things are respectful in their pastures
and only argue over if it's best
to let the snow melt or to make it melt.
Vapours turn to rainbows and are praised
while flowers breathe out oxygen for days.
Wait, am I thinking of the internet?
Oh, maybe not, but what I'm thinking of
is desperate and very, very like it.
I have in mind new forms of intimacy
that sadly elude me and huddle with
the young. Across the distances they hum
like snow leopards and pandas falling in love.

Michele Leggott

what is

it might be very early

it might be very late

fleecy marble the world

curve sticks out of

love's proper sphere

at the feet of the rider

stolen away for love

smoke touches the square

of the winged horse

and the lightfield explodes

blue flame and white

one handstand

for love stolen away

from the sooty altars

Anna Livesey

Autumn Day
(after Rilke)

The summer has gone on
past the point of expectation.
In the afternoons now, the ngaio
shades the fish pond.
Soon the first autumn wind
will gust up from the harbour.

It is time for us to gather
the last small peaches;
for the currants to ripen against the fence,
another day or two
pressing sweetness into the fruit.

She who has left us will not come now.
If we see her at all
it will be by chance, among dry leaves,
and she will not know us.

Bill Manhire

Huia

I was the first of birds to sing
I sang to signal rain
the one I loved was singing
and singing once again

My wings were made of sunlight
my tail was made of frost
my song was now a warning
and now a song of love

I sang upon a postage stamp
I sang upon your coins
but money courted beauty
you could not see the joins

Where are you when you vanish?
Where are you when you're found?
I'm made of greed and anguish
a feather on the ground

+

I lived among you once
and now I can't be found
I'm made of things that vanish
a feather on the ground

Kevin

I don't know where the dead go, Kevin.
The one far place I know
is inside the heavy radio. If I listen late at night,
there's that dark, celestial glow,
heaviness of the cave, the hive.

Music. Someone warms his hands at the fire,
breaking off the arms of chairs,
breaking the brute bodies of beds, burning his comfort
surely to keep alive. Soon he can hardly see,
and so, quietly, he listens: then someone lifts him
and it's some terrible breakfast show.

There are mothers and fathers, Kevin, whom we barely know.
They lift us. Eventually we all shall go
into the dark furniture of the radio.

Gregory O'Brien

Song

My Best Blue Suit
is now in
                   shreds
buttonholes
large enough for a 747

to fly through
sleeves you could
hitch a ride out of
     in any
               direction
and never find your way back
my best blue

     tattered suit
at a thousand loose ends
but baby
still my best
     very best
     blue suit.

Bob Orr

Song to Chelsea Wharf

When the sugar boat berths
at Chelsea wharf
a thousand wasps wait like stevedores.
A crane dips its finger
into the cavern of a hold
and then once again
as if it cannot quite believe the taste of tropical Australia.
How often have I watched
a sugar boat
steam out beneath the eyebrow of Auckland Harbour Bridge
into the dark pupil of this ocean.
Chelsea wharf
the sea gnaws at your piles
with rotten teeth
but tomorrow
I will stir you
into
     my cup
          of coffee.

Vincent O'Sullivan

The sentiment of goodly things

The birds are back at the feeder
now the air is warmer.
                    They come and go
in a way reminding me of keys in old
typewriters, flitting up and there for a second,
gone as another arrives.
                    I don't quite
catch at what it is they're typing,
something, once fancies, about enjoying
the fact of *again* and *again*.
                    I hope that's
what they're writing. It must be,
the way the keys keep coming back.

essa may ranapiri
(Ngāti Raukawa, Te Arawa, Ngāti Pukeko, Clan Gunn)

Silence, Part 2
(for Rowley Habib, after Keri Hulme's 'Silence')

Where are your bones?
    My bones are inside the house,
    leaning against the cabinet
    —it's empty.
Where are your bones?
    My bones are off on a forty-day trip
    to the desert in hope
    that it rains.
Where are your bones?
    My bones are in the engines of one million motor vehicles
    all pumping their best chemicals into the atmosphere.
Where are your bones?
    If you take a right turn after McDonald's
    they'll be in the trough with the meat patties.
    I swear the pigs won't touch them at all.
Where are your bones?
    My bones are drowning inside my bones.
Where are your bones?
    Being used by swimming teams
    to break into the changing rooms.
Where are your bones?
    The clatter the hit of my bones rings
    around the stadium, my bones breaking
    other bones
    my bones breaking windows, my bones
    stealing televisions and radios and all manner of extension cords.
Where are your bones?
    None of them long enough to connect back. To my real bones.

Where are your bones?
  Those bones that karakia those bones that can stand tall on the
  marae them bones that never dry out that always know what's up
  when it's up.
Where are your bones?
  My bones are eating my other bones and those other bones just want
  to go home.

Michael Steven

After Trakl

A fool's vision of frost an hour from dawn:

dew on the shed roof reflects back
what's left of last night's
moon.
                The sun will be rising soon,
and cicadas starting up again.
It's true.
        They own the stage
for most of the day,
lost in the heat of the dance.

Lately, though, with the sun falling earlier,
the evenings growing longer
and a little cooler,
                right on dusk
the crickets unpack their reed instruments
from dark leather cases

and belt out a few plangent notes.

Hone Tuwhare
(Ngāpuhi)

Haiku (1)

Stop
your snivelling
creek-bed:

come rain hail
and flood-water

laugh again

Haiku (1)
[Translated by Selwyn Muru]

Kāti
tō whenguwhengu mai
e te moenga o te awa:

piki mai e te ua
e te ua nganga
e te waipuke

kata kata mai ana rā

Rain

I can hear you
making small holes
in the silence
rain

If I were deaf
the pores of my skin
would open to you
and shut

And I
should know you
by the lick of you
if I were blind

the something
special smell of you
when the sun cakes
the ground

the steady
drum-roll sound
you make
when the wind drops

But if I
should not hear
smell or feel or see
you

you would still
define me
disperse me
wash over me
rain

Ua [Translated by Patu Hohepa]

Ka rongo au i a koe
e hanga kōwhao iti ana
i te marino
e ua

Mēnā he turi ahau
ka puare aku kōputa
ki a koe
ā, ka kati

Ko hau hoki
me taunga ki a koe
ki tō miti mai
me i kāpō ahau

ka pā mai
tō kakara rere kē
anō nei he whenua
i toka i te rā

ka mau tonu
te rongo o te tangi pahū
i a koe
me ka mutu te hau

Engari ina kore au
e rongo
e hongi e pā e kite
i a koe

ka riro tonu māu
e iriiri i ahau
e wehe i ahau
e horoi rawa i ahau
e ua.

Sun o (2)

Gissa smile Sun, giss yr best
good mawnin' one, fresh 'n cool like

yore still comin'—still
half in an' half outa the lan'scape?

An' wen yore clear of that eastern rim
of hills an' tha whole length of tha

valley begins to flood wit yr light, well
that's wen I could just reach out 'n stroke

tha pitted pock-marked pores of yr shiny
skin an' peel ya—just like an orange, right

down to yr white under-skin, but I wouldn't
bite ya—well, not until the lunch-bell goes

at noon wen I can feel ya hot an' outa reach
an' balanced right there—above my head.

C'mon, gissa smile Sun.

Oscar Upperton

Child's First Dictionary
(for Tess)

White flowers and red berries
means ghost notes in the attic.

A chicken in a cat cage
means horribly rising static.

New lambs buried in the garden
means love has come to stay.

Passionfruit cut on the vine
means trim the old bouquet.

Witchy foxglove fingers
means history has touched you.

Cats asleep on bunk beds
means turn the earth anew.

My pine-tree house, your pine-tree house,
means disturbed summer rest.

Rabbit bones under the pig house
means the autumn trees are blessed.

The nail caught in your knee that day
means things are not as I remember.
For me it was September.
For you it was December.

Richard von Sturmer

Baso is Unwell

Sun-faced Buddha:
persimmon
pineapple
papaya.

Moon-faced Buddha:
syringe
stethoscope
scalpel.

While on the bedside table
a glass of water holds
the early morning light.

From Sparrow Notebook

hey you sparrows!
I'm in my brown robe
where shall we go?

Bryan Walpert

Song

A river of geese rises
from the lake, their lift

the life of a breeze
or a boy, who stands

in the rain that shakes
from the trees

and thinks of a girl,
a leaf in the light,

day turning from night
and into the air, a care

or the hint of first snow.
Maybe he's been there,

standing all night,
letting stars streak

his lashes until
mountains appear

on the horizon's new air,
outlines of ships

or of fears. The birds
left their lake as flat

as a plain; water like
light has filled in the holes

left by geese in the rain,
which has ceased.

Ian Wedde

Abat-jour
(for Bill Culbert)

If you turn the light on
to look at it, you can't see it

because it's too bright. When you turn it off,
you can't see it because it's not

there. Look at the shadow, then,
see both what is and what might be.

From Shadow Stands Up

6.

I get up early hoping
I'll encounter the line drawn
under *night time*, the red streak
that bisects the shadow of
dawn standing up, horizon
of dark buildings in the east
whose windows begin to flash,
the gassy aquamarine
sky pouring itself into
the gaps between high-rise glass,
laser-streaks of gulls lit by
the afterburn of early
sunrise over there where hope
appears inevitable
and unwise, but worth getting
up early enough for, to
remember why you do this.

18.

What happens to memory
when the house is emptied, where
have they all gone, those sunlit
people by the wide windows,
table and chairs whose lunch-time
shadows the patient dog lay
down in, where has the music gone,
the sound of the front door
opening, who's coming in,
what will happen to them when
the door closes on empty
room, on an empty body
which lights fills without casting
the shadows of what we know?

Briar Wood
(Ngāpuhi Nui Tonu)

Paddle Crab

Nobody can get past you—
like a goalie you patrol
with a defensive wild sidestep
a war prance haka, tideline dance.

Gloved fist pincers raised,
limbs waving in challenge,
you can vanish in seconds
digging air holes, tunnelling,

crustacean talk, eyes on stalks,
poking out above the waves.
Scary Mister Jittery please
don't nibble my toes

for walking on your beach
or pinch my bum for swimming
in your water. After dark
the shoreline is all yours.

Whenua,
Moana,
Rangi

—

Earth,
Sea,
Sky

James K. Baxter

Blow, wind of fruitfulness

Blow, wind of fruitfulness
　　Blow from the buried sun:
Blow from the buried kingdom
　　Where heart and mind are one.

Blow, wind of fruitfulness,
　　The murmuring leaves remember;
For deep in doorless rock
　　Awaits their green September.

Blow from the wells of night:
　　The blind flower breathes thy coming
Birds that are silent now
　　And buds of barren springing.

Blow from beyond our day.
　　The hill-born streams complain;
Hear from their stony courses
　　The great sea rise again.

Blow on the mouth of morning
　　Renew the single eye:
And from remembered darkness
　　Our immortality.

Ursula Bethell

Detail

My garage is a structure of excessive plainness,
It springs from a dry bank in the back garden,
It is made of corrugated iron,
And painted all over with brick-red.

But beside it I have planted a green Bay-tree,
—A sweet Bay, an Olive, and a Turkey Fig,
—A Fig, an Olive, and a Bay.

Time

'Established' is a good word, much used in garden books,
'The plant, when established' . . .
Oh, become established quickly, quickly, garden
For I am fugitive, I am very fugitive — — —

Those that come after me will gather these roses,
And watch, as I do now, the white wistaria
Burst, in the sunshine, from its pale green sheath.

Planned. Planted. Established. Then neglected,
Till at last the loiterer by the gate will wonder
At the old, old cottage, the old wooden cottage,
And say 'One might build here, the view is glorious;
This must have been a pretty garden once.'

Ben Brown
(Ngāti Paoa, Ngāti Mahuta)

Pūriri

Pūriri
Tree of the dead
Of the green moth
And the tortured limb
Tree of anger
Tree of peace
Unruly in aspect
Unlike a kauri
Which has majesty

Pūriri
Defiant and silent
Hollowed when old
A place to hide
Outside my present window
A tūī inhabits the branches
Noisy bugger wakes me
In the morning

Alistair Te Ariki Campbell

The Return

And again I see the long pouring headland,
And smoking coast with the sea high on the rocks,
The gulls flung from the sea, the dark hooded hills
Swarming with mist, and mist low on the sea.

And on the surf-loud beach the long spent hulks,
The mats and splintered masts, the fires kindled
On the wet sand, and men moving between the fires,
Standing or crouching with backs to the sea.

Their heads finely shrunken to a skull, small
And delicate, with small black rounded beaks;
Their antique bird-like chatter bringing to mind
Wild locusts, bees, and trees filled with wild honey —

And, sweet as incense-clouds, the smoke rising, the fire
Spitting with rain, and mist low with rain —
Their great eyes glowing, their rain-jewelled, leaf-green
Bodies leaning and talking with the sea behind them:

Plant gods, tree gods, gods of the middle world . . . Face downward
And in a small creek mouth all unperceived,
The drowned Dionysus, sand in his eyes and mouth,
In the dim tide lolling — beautiful, and with the last harsh

Glare of divinity from lip and broad brow ebbing . . .
The long-awaited! And the gulls passing over with shrill cries;
And the fires going out on the thundering sand;
And the mist, and the mist moving over the land.

Geoff Cochrane

Our City and Its Hills
(for Bill)

The steampunk city's Buddhist rain
Is marvellously hushed
It always thus affects my brain
And stops me getting lushed

The steampunk city's Buddhist rain
Wets rooftop flue and tank
It makes me want to catch a train
And ride through cuttings dank

The steampunk city's Buddhist rain
Is not unkind to cats
It falls on cenotaph and crane
And blackens many hats

Some put their faith in sleeping-pills
Or brash domestic wines,
But the rain has altars in the hills
And cloisters in the pines,
The rain has altars in the hills
And cloisters in the pines

The Sea the Landsman Knows
(for Rod Hall)

The sea the landsman knows, saltless and blue,
Denies the death at its deep green bottom;

Denies that dark heave of menace
You pilot your sleeping skipper through,

Perched above a thumping marine V.8.,
Your fingers the gimbals of a lodestone heart.

Shipping life, we founder,
But liquor makes us buoyant,

So here's to the faceless, mooning drowned
Who dream forever of anchors and mermaids

Where fish-shaped fish and shower-curtain seaweeds
Bubble transparency skyward, and are never rained on.

Ruth Dallas

Milking before Dawn

In the drifting rain the cows in the yard are as black
And wet and shiny as rocks in an ebbing tide;
But they smell of the soil, as leaves lying under trees
Smell of the soil, damp and steaming, warm.
The shed is an island of light and warmth, the night
Was water-cold and starless out in the paddock.

Crouched on the stool, hearing only the beat
The monotonous beat and hiss of the smooth machines,
The choking gasp of the cups and rattle of hooves,
How easy to fall asleep again, to think
Of the man in the city asleep; he does not feel
The night encircle him, the grasp of mud.

But now the hills in the east return, are soft
And grey with mist, the night recedes, and the rain.
The earth as it turns towards the sun is young
Again, renewed, its history wiped away
Like the tears of a child. Can the earth be young again
And not the heart? Let the man in the city sleep.

Eileen Duggan

The Tides Run up the Wairau

The tides run up the Wairau
That fights against their flow.
My heart and it together
Are running salt and snow.

For though I cannot love you,
Yet, heavy, deep, and far,
Your tide of love comes swinging,
Too swift for me to bar.

Some thought of you must linger,
A salt of pain in me,
For oh what running river
Can stand against the sea?

David Eggleton

Edgeland

Awks: you winged Auk-thing, awkward, huddling;
you wraparound, myriad, amphibious,
stretchy, try-hard, Polywoodish
juggernaut; you futurescape, insectivorous,
Ākarana, Aukalani, Jafaville, O for Awesome,
still with the land-fever of a frontier town—

your surveyors who tick location, location, location,
your land-sharks, your swamp-lawyers, your merchant kings,
your real-estate agents who bush-bash for true north,
your architecture that fell off the back of a truck,
your shoebox storerooms of apartment blocks,
your subdivisions sticky as pick and mix lollies;
you fat-bellied hybrid with your anorexic anxieties,
your hyperbole and bulimia, your tear-down and throw-up,
the sands of your hourglass always replenished,
your self-harm always rejuvenated, unstoppable;
you binge-drinker, pre-loader, storm-chaser,
mana-muncher, hui-hopper, waka-jumper,

light opera queen, the nation's greatest carnivore;
cloud-city of the South Pacific, it's you the lights adore.

Rangi Faith
(Kāi Tahu, Ngāti Kahungunu)

Karakia to a Silent Island

How do I greet you, motutapu?
How do I call across the darkness,
fish your still waters?

On what ears
do these words fall
& who is left to speak
for the tangatawhenua,
for the ghosts on the beach?

How do I greet you, motutapu?
How do I feel your pain,
your battlewounds?
Where man has fed on man,
how do I celebrate whanau?

As my canoe glides
through your silence –
only this –
kia ora ki a koe,
kia ora, kia ora, kia ora.

Spring star

My dog howls
at the sea booming
over the
windthrown pines;
he is not alone.
Pūkekos scream
in the spring
darkness;
it is the time
of the star
across the moon,
it is time
for the sighting
of new mountains.

Denis Glover

Home Thoughts

I do not dream of Sussex downs
or quaint old England's
quaint old towns –
I think of what may yet be seen
in Johnsonville or Geraldine.

Threnody

In Plimmerton, in Plimmerton,
The little penguins play,
And one dead albatross was found
At Karehana Bay.

In Plimmerton, in Plimmerton,
The seabirds haunt the cave,
And often in the summertime
The penguins ride the wave.

In Plimmerton, in Plimmerton,
The penguins live, they say,
But one dead albatross they found
At Karehana Bay.

The Magpies

When Tom and Elizabeth took the farm
The bracken made their bed,
And *Quardle oodle ardle wardle doodle*
The magpies said.

Tom's hand was strong to the plough
Elizabeth's lips were red,
And *Quardle oodle ardle wardle doodle*
The magpies said.

Year in year out they worked
While the pines grew overhead,
And *Quardle oodle ardle wardle doodle*
The magpies said.

But all the beautiful crops soon went
To the mortgage-man instead,
And *Quardle oodle ardle wardle doodle*
The magpies said.

Elizabeth is dead now (it's years ago);
Old Tom went light in the head;
And *Quardle oodle ardle wardle doodle*
The magpies said.

The farm's still there. Mortgage corporations
Couldn't give it away.
And *Quardle oodle ardle wardle doodle*
The magpies say.

Dinah Hawken

Drama

The lake is grey and speechless, in a state
of glimmer and rarely seen light.

Don't disturb it with wishful thinking,
it has *become* wishful thinking.

Think of dreaming, drowning, sleep.
Or just don't think.

A coot, up and over, has gone inside it
barely leaving a trace.

Will I ever learn to let it be, this graceful,
windless, windowless lake?

Jeffrey Paparoa Holman

From The Late Great Blackball Bridge Sonnets

xxiii.

In the house of my body I carry that river.
In the depths of my being I'm water. My

body's the home of a wandering miner
too old to go down and too tired to go on.

When I stand on the world and look over
what's living, what's left, I'm the bridge

to the past and the road still unfolding.
Wheels and water, tracks and steam, all

the footprints beside the river, thousands
of hours spent double in blackness, a light

on my head to remind me I'm human. In
the shape of my bones I'm an NZR sleeper

and when my last shift comes, my Dog Watch
boys, lay me like coal by the sea at Karoro.

Keri Hulme

(Kāi Tahu, Ngāti Māmoe, Nordic, Celtic)

The Wine-Rich Arteries

The rain is falling in my head
it lilts the rhythm of the dead
                        haere haere ki te po
the rain is falling in my heart

the sun is shining in my mind
it blinds the memories that I find
                        haere haere ki te po
the sun is burning up my heart

the wind is blowing in my bones
it tries to dry the sap to stone
                        haere haere ki te po
          it seeks the wine-rich arteries
          all the sweet and pulsing parts
          all the debris of my heart
and whines to set them free:
whistle, wind, for futility
                        haere haere ki te po

Robin Hyde

The Last Ones

But the last black horse of all
Stood munching the green-bud wind,
And the last of the raupo huts
Let down its light behind.
Sullen and shadow-clipped
He tugged at the evening star,
New-mown silvers swished like straw
Across the manuka.

As for the hut, it said
No word but its meagre light,
Its people slept as the dead,
Bedded in Maori night.
'And there is the world's last door,
And the last world's horse,' sang the wind,
'With little enough before,
And what you have seen behind.'

Cilla McQueen

Out the Black Window
(for Ralph)

out the black window
into reflections, a rosary

it is clear
night is already in the hedge
& under the rainwater tank

the trees rust, the squeaky birds
sing tootle tootle wick wick wick
& power poles are lighting up
with children's voices

bicycle
wheel
whizz

the lonely dog under the tree
barks for his master to come home to the brick house.

macrocarpa trundles big black arms,
a heavy witch galumphing around the graveyard

& an insistent one note thrush
chips, the birdsong
swings like a coathanger.

Karlo Mila

Manuhiri

in the Manawatu
pine needles stitch together
a patchwork of green pastures
oh those pines
they're everywhere you go
We're not exotic anymore they argue
We have roots here too they say
Ask that old guy on One Tree Hill
and Tane Mahuta's laughing

John Newton

Beetle

Out of the dusk, through the open
window and onto this lit plane of paper tumbles

a brown beetle, a winged chip of warmth,
of November. Outside

now in the softness
you can feel them mustering furrily under your toes

and the trout which are feeding viciously
fattening up after that famous winter

go crazy, or that's what they'll tell you, anyhow,
and all down the river

the cherries are bulging in the orchards now while this
horny little beetle

cranks up its wings and spins frantic 360s the size
of a bottletop, buzzing.

Bob Orr

Song to Rangitoto

There are no bells
beyond Rangitoto . . . out there the hands of fishermen
return to the sea.
Moutihe is a casket of sailors' bones
watched over by seagulls
Motutapu is a miniature Australia
Tiritiri Matangi a taniwha
whose lighthouse eye scans shipping lanes
but Rangitoto is the island that has always frightened me.
Funeral urn and chalice
you have something in common
with the funnels of departing ships.
On Monday
a sailor sings your solitude
on Tuesday
cloud shadows spend an afternoon with you
on Wednesday
Mission Bay wonders why you have no ice-cream parlours
(it would though wouldn't it?)
on Thursday
a storm bares its teeth at you
on Friday
the pubescent cones of Devonport keep their distance from you
on Saturday
a ship girl counts the trinkets of your channel beacons
on Sunday
the Harbour Bridge
the ghost of your double
as insubstantial as the blueprint of a gannet's wing
has dreams to one day fly away with you –
on some lost day in between
I find your silhouette tattooed across my heart's north-east.

Beneath the plumb line of a star
your nine letters make an island afloat on the ocean.
A tuft of cigarette smoke streams out seaward from my window.
This logbook
I am
keeping
with a feather that is burning.

Kiri Piahana-Wong
(Ngāti Ranginui, Chinese, English)

After the sun

After the sun has
set, it seems
impossible that it
could ever rise
again.

Night
sinks into the
bones.

The cliff face
looks weary.
The sand is hard
and cold. The
ocean curls around
its secrets.

Elizabeth Smither

Here come the clouds

Here come the clouds the same as last June
Puffy like the breasts of birds, one . . . two . . . three . . .
They have circumnavigated the world
Birds heavy from flight, home again.

A year has passed. Now they fill the sky
Thicker and thicker having no other place to go.
What is the end of navigation then? They seem
Swollen as though their arteries of air

Ached from memory as well and
Dilated their hearts so they come
Weighed with longing for their homeland.
And here they are. Is this it then?
This empty sky, waiting.

Brian Turner

From Faces in the Water

There was a track
through the willows
to the river
where it arrowed
into a long
deep pool.

In the evenings
trout sipped
spent spinners
in the fading light
as the sky came down
like a wall.

*

In the afternoons
the mountains
far off
in realms of sleep,

the sheep and cattle
lying down,
and thick grass
springy and tall

noisy with insects
along the banks
of the river
reflecting the sky.

*

Swing slow,
ripple
then run,

talk on
then break
into song,

long river.
river long
gone.

Hone Tuwhare
(Ngāpuhi)

Reign rain

Neither juggernaut
man
nor crawling thing
with saintliness and ease

can bring
a mountain weeping
to its knees
quicker than rain:

that demure leveller
ocean-blessed
cloud-sent
maker of plains.

Ūa uaua [Translated by Patu Hohepa]

Hore he mea horonuku
tangata
mea ngaoki whenua rānei
mā te āhua hāto me te ngāwari

e whakaheke
maunga tangi
ki ōna turi
horo atu i te ua:

tēnā kaiwhakamaene mārire
tā te moana tohu
tononga a kapua
kaihanga mānia.

Briar Wood
(Ngāpuhi Nui Tonu)

Paewai o te Moana

The sea at night is blacklit,
kikorangi, kōura, topazerine, pango,
a haul of images pouring from nets,
darker than oil underground

at the edge of Parawhenuamea
rave streams, jostling yachts,
brown iris flags, meadowfoam, puka

Tai Timu, Tai Pari, arawhata ki

pocket beaches of pebble shell rock
meaning a joining of waka
across the slanted playing field

virtual beaches on imaginary roads
where poetry and geometry are almost
compatible, wai weld, creolerie,

ocean patter in ngā kupu,
tūātea, ngaru mata, rahopē

moana waiwai, karma moana,
beforeglow and sonar,

like finding

whakaea

Love Songs

Fleur Adcock

Comment

The four-year-old believes he likes
vermouth; the cat eats cheese;
and you and I, though scarcely more
convincingly than these,
walk in the gardens, hand in hand,
beneath the summer trees.

Te Awhina Rangimarie Arahanga

(Rapuwai, Waitaha, Ngāti Māmoe, Ngāi Tahu)

Pohutukawa Plays the Blues

Let's run away
retreat
chill out, mate
on the nook
of the crook
on the branch
of the trunk
where the woman
in olive and red
shrouds and captures hues
Where sea beats a slow
constant rhythm
insects hum and buzz
We can throw
our bodies down
stretch out
sweaty toes
pull our palms
beneath heads
to yearn
while lady above
plays the blues

Nick Ascroft

Corpse Seeks Similar

Here, in the A & E
I am billowing
With thoughts of romance.

I would like to meet someone
With a broken shoulder or
Half-crazed with psychosomatic tinnitus.

I would like
To meet someone who would know
The meaning of pain &

Wouldn't curdle like
A milky child when
I contaminate them with my affections,

Who wouldn't double up or squeal
Like a castrated pig when
I gore them with my personality.

Here, as my body deserts me
In a pool at my feet,
As I slur sweet nothings

At the nurses, passing like white buses,
I would like to find you,
My future beloved,

Perhaps you, there,
Draped over those crutches, there,
Eyes rolled back in the corner, there,

I would like to meet you,
Hold your bandaged hand &
Pass out with you.

Hinemoana Baker

(Ngāti Raukawa, Ngāti Toa Rangatira, Te Ātiawa, Ngāi Tahu,
German, English)

Matariki, e

you have gone home

you made me feel
I had discovered fire

you have left the room

you made me feel
I had invented the wheel

in the end
room   we gather
round you

you made me feel
the sun wheeled in me
the moon on my tongue

Serie Barford

A matter of time

the living sing
so do the dead

I should know
my dreams are operas

a phantom lali
beats time

a countdown

we will be together again

hand on heart

promise

Ursula Bethell

Compensation

I went down into the trivial city to transact business.
In the tramcar passengers argued without logic;
In the shops too costly wares;
In the Bank too little money;
In the long streets too hot sun.

But at the Post Office they gave me your letter.
In my hill garden at sunset I read it.
A cool wind from the seawaves blew gently
And I saw that little Omi-Kin-Kan had put forth a green shoot.

Hera Lindsay Bird

I have come back from the dead to tell you that I love you

I have come to move your cups transparently through the air
To tremble in the corner of your eye like a fuzzy diamond

I am shaking off my worms like cowboy tassels!!!
I have put your bedsheet over my head and cut both eyeholes out

Lilacs, snakes, disco-balls, birdbaths
Alligators, tennis courts, self-respect, nothing

Green tin roofs shining all along the river
& the palliative stars above

I lie underground, sprouting flowers like a rural Liberace
my tumours like pink bells ringing into oblivion,

I have come back one last time to look at you
Your beauty is heavy on my eyes, like tiny anvils

I have come back to our house on the last day of summer
I have come back to say I love you, and I'm sorry for being dead

Peter Bland

The cabin

'Love is that you remain standing
In front of your Beloved.'
— Al Hallaj

Are you there, my love, my one
true darling? How fleetingly
a shared lifetime passed!
(It was water slipping
through cupped hands.) I know
it's too late – isn't it
always – but I've built
a small cabin in the space
you've left. You'd be
hugely at home there. It's
full of wine and song. I suppose
it's a sort of halfway house
where lovers can learn
to live as strangers
as well as coming together
as one. Perhaps
shared alonenesses
are what love's about?
Anyway it's there and it's waiting
should you ever walk this way again.

Behrouz Boochani

Forgive me my love

[Translated by Moones Mansoubi, Manus Island,
Papua New Guinea, 2018]

Forgive me my bird as I am not able to embrace you.
But here,
in this corner,
I know some migrating birds that I smile to at dawn.
I embrace them with open arms,
as open as the immensity of the sky.

My beautiful love!
Forgive me as I am not able to drink the aroma of your
     breath,
but here, in the ruins of this prison,
wildflowers grow each morning in my heart
and in the dead of night they drift into sleep with me,
     where I rest.

Forgive me my angel!
As I am not able to caress your gentle skin with my
     fingertips.
But I have a lifelong friendship with the zephyr
and those gentle winds from the sea strum my bare skin
     here in this tropical purgatory.

Forgive me, as I am not able to climb the verdant
     mountains of your body,
but here, in the depths of darkness, always at midnight, I
     enjoy deep and utter seclusion
among the tall and dignified coconut trees.

My beautiful! I sing to you the profundities of the most
    ancient and enigmatic songs,
far away from the world, a man loves you from within the
    deepest oceans and the darkest forests.
Inside a cage,
the man loves you,
inside a cage located between the vastest ocean and the
    densest jungle . . .

Forgive me my love as I am solely able to love you from a
    remote island,
inside a cage,
from the corner of this small room.

Forgive me please as the only part of the world that belongs
    to me are these fragments.

Jenny Bornholdt

Wedding song

Now you are married
try to love the world
as much as you love
each other. Greet it as your husband,
wife. Love it with all your
might as you sleep
breathing against its back.

Love the world, when, late at night,
you come home to find snails
stuck to the side of the house
like decoration.

Love your neighbours.
The red berries on their trampoline
their green wheelbarrow.

Love the man walking on
water, the man up a
mast. Love the light moving
across the *Island Princess*.

Love your grandmother when she tells you
her hair is three-quarters 'cafe au lait'.

Try to love the world, even when you discover
there is no such thing as *The Author*
any more.

Love the world, praise
god, even, when your aerobics instructor
is silent.

Try very hard to love
your mailman, even though he regularly
delivers you Benedicto Clemente's mail.

Love the weta you find on the path,
injured by alteration.

Love the tired men, the burnt
house, the handlebars of light
on the ceiling.

Love the man on the bus who says
it all amounts to a fishing rod
or a light bulb.

Love the world of the garden.
The keyhole of bright green grass
where the stubborn palm
used to be,
bees so drunk on ginger flowers
that they think the hose water
is rain   your hair tangled in
heartsease.   Love the way,
when you come inside,
insects find their way out
from the temporary rooms of
your clothes.

Bub Bridger
(Ngāti Kahungunu, Irish, English)

Wild daisies

If you love me
bring me flowers
wild daisies
clutched in your fist
like a torch
no orchids or roses
or carnations
no florist's bow
just daisies
steal them
risk your life for them
up the sharp hills
in the teeth of the wind
if you love me
bring me daisies
wild daisies
that I will cram
in a bright vase
and marvel at

Robbie Burns

To Mary in Heaven

Thou lingering star, with lessening ray
That lovest to greet the early morn,
Again thou usherest in the day
My Mary from my soul was torn.
O Mary! Dear, departed Shade!
Where is thy place of blissful rest?
Seest thou thy lover lowly laid?
Hear'st thou the groans that rend his breast?

That sacred hour can I forget,
Can I forget the hallowed grove,
Where by the winding Ayr, we met,
To live one day of Parting Love?
Eternity can not efface
Those records dear of transports past;
Thy image at our last embrace,
Ah! little thought we 'twas our last!

Ayr gurgling kiss'd his pebbled shore,
O'erhung with wild-woods, thickening green;
The fragrant birch, and hawthorn hoar,
Twined, am'rous, round the raptured scene:
The flowers sprang wanton to be prest,
The birds sang love on every spray;
Till too, too soon the glowing west
Proclaimed the speed of winged day.

Still o'er these scenes my mem'ry wakes,
And fondly broods with miser-care;
Time but th' impression stronger makes,
As streams their channels deeper wear,
My Mary! dear departed shade!

Where is thy place of blissful rest!
See'st thou thy Lover lowly laid!
Hear'st thou the groans that rend his breast!

Ki a Meri i Te Rangi [Translated by Rēweti Kōhere]

E koe e te whetu morehu, e korekoreko atu ra,
Ko tau i aroha ai ko te powhiri i te ata tu,
Ko taua ra tenei e uakina mai nei e koe
I takiritia atu ai taku Meri i toku uma.
Aue, e Meri! e te atarangi arohaina kua rere!
Kei hea ra tou wahi okiokitanga o te koa?
E kite ranei koe i tau 'ipo e roha nei?
E rongo ranei koe i te hotu e haehae nei i tona uma?

E wareware koia i a au taua haora tapu,
E wareware koia i a au te urupuia rahui
I tutaki ai taua i Aea pikopiko,
Kia noho mo te ra kotahi o te aroha tauwehe!
E kore ra e memeha mo ake tonu atu
Nga hotunga o taua ngakau o ia ra;
Tou whakaahua i te awhi whakamutunga:
Aue! kihai taua i mahara he awhi tauwehe!

Ko Aea, wawa tonu, aumiri tonu i ona paranga onepu,
Taumaru tonu iho nga ngahere, matomato tonu;
Ko te kohe kakara me te kareo mumura,
Aroha tonu te tauawhi i taua wahi miharo:
Ko nga puawai titiro ake ana kia katohia,
Ta nga manu he waiata aroha i nga manga:
Hohoro tonu ia te ura mai o te uru,
He whakaatu ra e topa ana te ra ki tona tauranga.
Ko toku ngakau ia e kore rawa e wareware,
Ko taku kai he mamae he pouri;
Ko ta te wa he whakahohonu i te mahara,

Me nga wai rere e keri nei i te oneone,
E taku Meri! e te atarangi arohaina kua rere!
Kei hea ra tou wahi okiokitanga o te koa?
E kite ranei koe i tau 'ipo e roha nei?
E rongo ranei koe i te hotu e haehae nei i tona uma?

Alistair Te Ariki Campbell

Roots

The wind blew hard again today,
tried to blow away my poems,
but to no avail,
for they had sunk their roots
deep into the hillside,
deep into the stones, the grass,
the trees, the songs of birds,
the light on land and sea
that never dies,
the light in your eyes.

Jacq Carter
(Ngāti Awa, Ngāi Te Rangi, English, Irish)

E noho rā

Let my body
bear the traces
of your passage
over me

like the land
of our ancestors
bears the tracks
of their feet.

Let my face
bear the lines
of our passage
through time

the layers
of our knowing
etched like thin
blue lines.

Let my heart
bear the rhythm
of the passage
of my blood

as it swells
with the call
a karanga
to my love . . .

E noho rā, Tongariro
E noho rā, Te Taupō-nui-a-Tia
E noho rā, Tūwharetoa

Me tū tahi ahau
hai mānuka

Me tū tahi ahau
hai mānuka.

Glenn Colquhoun

A spell refusing to consider the mending of a broken heart

Consider the wounds under water.
Consider how mountains are torn.
Consider the holes in volcanoes.
Consider how old men are born.

Consider the sun is still burning.
Consider the branching of trees.
Consider the autumn in springtime.
Consider the falling of leaves.

Consider the gaps in the evening.
Consider the bend in the moon.
Consider the lining of faces.
Consider the dent in a spoon.

Consider the breaking of oceans.
Consider the lean on a mast.
Consider the crack inside lightning
And always leave open your heart.

Ruth Dallas

A Girl's Song

When love came
           glancing
                    down our street
Scarlet leaves
        flew
           round our feet,

      sang the girl, sewing.

He told me
        he would
                come again
Before
      the avenue
           turned green,

sang the girl, sewing.

How could I know,
           or guess,
                till now
The sadness
      of a
         summer bough,

      sang the girl, sewing.

Eileen Duggan

The Bushfeller

Lord, mind your trees to-day!
My man is out there clearing.
God send the chips fly safe.
My heart is always fearing.

And let the axehead hold!
My dreams are all of felling.
He earns our bread far back.
And then there is no telling.

If he came home at nights,
We'd know, but it is only—
We might not even hear—
A man could lie there lonely.

God, let the trunks fall clear,
He did not choose his calling;
He's young and full of life—
A tree is heavy, falling.

Bernadette Hall

Living out here on the plains
(for John)

through thick and thin
      through storm and shine

my hand on your heart, yours on mine,
      we'll try to keep our weather fine

just see, the city folk will say,
      how coolly they have abandoned

their language
      in the face of progress

Nicole Titihuia Hawkins
(Ngāti Kahungunu ki Te Wairoa, Ngāti Pāhauwera)

He piko

This love is a wide river
that lives in my puku,
a taniwha at each bend,
calm and deep
making its way
slowly to the sea

Sam Hunt

Porirua Friday Night

Acne blossoms scarlet on their cheeks,
These kids up Porirua East . . .
Pinned across this young girl's breast
A name-tag on the supermarket badge;
A city-sky-blue smock.
Her face unclenches like a fist.

Fourteen when I met her first
A year ago, she's now left school,
Going with the boy
She hopes will marry her next year.
I asked if she found it hard
Working in the store these Friday nights
When friends are on the town.

She never heard:
But went on, rather, talking of
The house her man had put
A first deposit on
And what it's like to be in love.

Kevin Ireland

Each day would end

where should I go
what do
there is nothing that matters
without you
not old
not new
not false
not true
there is nothing at all
without you

the days would have
not gloom nor glow
the wind would be
not fast nor slow
there is nothing that matters
that they could know
not friend
not foe
not joy
not woe
each day would end
the wind would blow
there is nothing at all
that they could know

the heart would be empty
the mind bare
the hand would lose
both fear and dare
there is nothing that matters
without you there

not curse
not prayer
not risk
not care
not fire nor water
not earth nor air
there is nothing at all
without you there

Anna Jackson

The treehouse

Not having known the child
I love his graveyard,

the man who has grown up
over the child's bones,

the hair that springs like grass
from his shoulder blades,

the rise and fall of him,
the archaeology I disturb

late at night, asking him
for a story, as if we lay awake

in a treehouse, shining a torch
into the forest around us,

losing the beam
in the dark.

Gregory Kan

[When you move]

When you move

a look moves inside me

and eats there what I eat.

Michele Leggott

wild light

this is the spring
of the world of light
te puna i te ao marama
diffused refracted irradiant
wild light
sitting there looking at me
making me remember
walking thought the world
travelling light
because our hearts
those crazy old caloyers
have gone on ahead
with all the stories on a string
all the stories in the world
waiting to happen
again
light swings between us
luminous and dispersive
anguish no anguish
I won't be back this way again
but the world of light
throws its salts into the sky
one more time
foam dew clouds lightning
and on this arm
of the harbouring planet
we look up and agree to live
in perpetual commotion
a new moon and just below it
the evening star

Jiaqiao Liu

to a future you

i.

This morning, the bus passed the corner store
with the Genji mural, and I was driven by some impulse
to look higher than myself. In the cold, flighty sun:
a sapling clinging to a concrete pillar.
a pōhutukawa in the crash of the CBD.
The bus stopped right below it.
I saw the bluest sky.

that hand is for holding
(after Jupiter)

I have
only what I have:
      a tiny snail shell
      a pitted pāua, a spray
      of baby's breath

and the kaleidoscopic cloudburst
I become
when left
      unsupervised in your presence

and anyway I left all that in the car
and all I really have is my body and its changes
and my narrow, unchanging heart
and my handfuls of chamomile
and honey
      I want
      to hold you
      by the eyeballs

Gregory O'Brien

A patriot of the time of day

Walking the dreams in and out of their
shabby costumes and ill-fitting wardrobes
    I am a patriot of the time of day
and you are the sparkling things apples
wear. Feathers will rise to greet you
clouds will pick crumbs off your collar

and angels scuffling out in the yard
for chickenfeed will slide graciously
    down each particle of dust.
Ferry captains will sail their vessels
softly up against you as sparrows fasten
themselves to trees and tears blow wildly

across your face. My ears will register
only the faintest murmur—a small flower
    telling a comet to tuck in its tail—
the angle of your hair will be an education
the taste of moonlight on shallow water
and I will feel the forms of your bones

as gently as the breath of a snail
as a memory of my grandmother at the
    beginning of the century riding
back to Hokitika in the dead of night
Halley's Comet trailing like a kite
behind the horse-drawn cart.

A Visiting Card

How lightly we
carry ourselves

that stirring in
the long grass yes

five minutes ago
that was us.

Joanna Margaret Paul

the dilettante

on Monday I was incurably ill
on Tuesday I talked all night
on Wednesday I slept all day
on Thursday I fell in love
on Friday I said goodbye
This was an extraordinary week
This was an ordinary week.

Ruby Solly
(Kāi Tahu, Waitaha, Kāti Māmoe)

How to Meet Your Future Husband in his Natural Habitat

You will find him
somewhere between the tallest tōtara,
and the deepest ocean.

Then he will press you,
hands first
into the moss beneath.

And as you fall,
you will hear the pūrerehua
summon the rains.

When they fall,
press your hands
further into his back.

Carve him new valleys,
sculpt mountain ranges from
his shoulders.

Exhale as you watch them
close the gap between sea
and sky.

Robert Sullivan
(Ngāpuhi, Kāi Tahu, Irish)

Arohanui

Big love, that's what it means.
Aroha Nunui means huge love.
Aroha Nunui Rawa means very huge love.
Aroha Nunui Rawa Ake means bigger very huge love.
Aroha Nunui Rawa Ake Tonu
      means bigger enduring very huge love.
Aroha Nunui Rawa Ake Tonu Atu
      means biggest enduring hugest love,
which are some of the lengths and times of our longing.

Paraire Hēnare Tomoana
(Ngāti Te Whatu-i-āpiti, Ngāti Kahungunu)

Pōkarekare ana

Pōkarekare ana ngā wai o Waiapu.
Whiti atu koe, e hine, marino ana ē!

E hine ē, hoki mai rā!
Ka mate ahau i te aroha ē!

E kore te aroha e maroke i te rā.
Mākūkū tonu i aku roimata ē!

E hine ē, hoki mai rā!
Ka mate ahau i te aroha ē!

Tuhituhi taku reta, tuku atu taku rīngi.
Kia kite tō iwī, raruraru ana ē!

E hine ē, hoki mai rā!
Ka mate ahau i te aroha ē!

Whatiwhati taku pene, kua pau aku pepa.
Ko taku aroha mau tonu ana ē!

E hine ē, hoki mai rā!
Ka mate ahau i te aroha ē!

[Translation] The Waters of Waiapu

Stormy are the waters of Waiapu.
If you cross them, girl, they will be calm.

Come back to me girl,
I am so much in love!

My love will never dry in the sun.
It will always be wet with my tears.

Come back to me girl,
I am so much in love!

I write my letter and send my ring.
If your people see them, there will be trouble.

Come back to me girl,
I am so much in love!

My pen is broken, my paper used up.
My love for you will always remain.

Come back to me girl,
I am so much in love!

Hone Tuwhare
(Ngāpuhi)

Nocturne

And if the earth should tremble
to the sea's unfathomed rage
it is because the sun has fled
uncupping the stone nipples
of the land.

The moon has torn
from the pulsing arm of the sea
a tawdry bracelet . . . and I
alone am left
with the abandoned earth
and the night-sea sobbing.

My heart shall limping come
to police the night
so that no surly light
shall flare
nor sad spring blood forth
a despond moon
to limn the swollen night
in anguish.

Oriori o Te Pō [Translated by Selwyn Muru]

Pēnā ka rū te whenua
i runga i te hōhonutanga o te riri a te moana
nā te mea kua oma te whakangaro te Rā
nāna nei i hurahura ngā titi kōhatu
o Papatūānuku.

Kia tītorehia e te marama
huri noa i te ringa kaha o Tangaroa
he kuru pounamu weriweri . . . Nā ināianei ko ahau
anake kua mahue mokemoke mai
ki runga i te panitanga (o te mata) o te whenua
ki ngā tai hoki e tangihotuhotu nei i te pō.

Ko taku manawa ka toti haere mai
ki te tiaki i te pō uriuri,
kia hore ai te kāpura parauri e muruake
Te puna wai pōuri rānei e whakatoto ake
i te marama ngoikore
ki te whakaahua i te teteretanga o te pō
me tēnā pōuri nui whakaharahara.

Albert Wendt

In Your Enigma
(for Reina)

You are dressed in your enigma
You shift like mist across words
that describe water
You plant signs
You invent yourself in syllables
of nightlight and winter turning
to spring on Maungawhau's shoulders

Every thing is
Every thing is earth the atua feed on
Every thing is earth moulded in Ruaumoko's belly
and thrown up to know
Tane's kiss of living air

Your ancestors left their shadows
for you to grow into
They fished islands and visions out
of tides that washed back into the Void
They dealt in imagery of bone and feather
They knew the alphabet of omens
and could cipher the silences
that once knew the speech of pain
They planted white pebbles in the mouths
of their dead and sailed them
into the eyes of the future

You are dressed in your enigma
that finds language in the gift
that is water
that is earth
that is every thing

Sue Wootton

Magnetic South

You are my magnetic south.
I fall to you true.

I am the eel, the gull,
the silvery fish,
returning and returning.

Yours is the tide I swim to.

Ngati Whakahemo

He Waiata Aroha

1.

Kāore te aroha e huri i runga rā o
Aku kiri kanohi, he hanga kia māpuna te
Roimata i aku kamo, ē.

2.

Me aha te aroha e mauru ai rā?
Mai ki pikitia te hira kai te Pare-o-Te-
Rawahirua, kia mihi atu au te
Ripa ki Matawhau'; nāku ia nā koe
Koi huri ki te tua, ī.

3.

Pere taku titiro te au kai te moana o
Tuhua i waho, he rerenga hipi mai
Nōhou, e Te Kiore, hei kawe i ahau ki
Tai o ngā muri, kei marutata 'hau te
Whakamau ki te iwi e.

A Song of Love [Translated by Pei Te Hurinui Jones]

1.

Always the longing is uppermost
And upon my eyelashes, bubbling forth,
Are the tears from mine eyes.

2.

How am I to abate this longing?
Let me ascend the lower brow of Pare-o-Te-
Rawahirua, where I might greet the
Current of Matawhau'; for it was I who
Turned my back on you.

3.

My gaze darts forth to the ocean current of
Tuhua out yonder, where comes sailing in the ships of
You, O Te Kiore, to take me to
The seas in the north, where I will draw nigh
And direct my way to the tribe.

Whānau

Fleur Adcock

For a Five-Year-Old

A snail is climbing up the window-sill
into your room, after a night of rain.
You call me in to see, and I explain
that it would be unkind to leave it there:
it might crawl to the floor; we must take care
that no one squashes it. You understand,
and carry it outside, with careful hand,
to eat a daffodil.

I see, then, that a kind of faith prevails:
your gentleness is moulded still by words
from me, who have trapped mice and shot wild birds,
from me, who drowned your kittens, who betrayed
your closest relatives, and who purveyed
the harshest kind of truth to many another.
But that is how things are: I am your mother,
and we are kind to snails.

Tusiata Avia

Helicopter

My mother told him
With all that money you could have bought a helicopter.
You could have packed them all in
    Cousins like corned beef
    Aunties like elegi
    Uncles like saimigi
    Brothers like taro
    Sisters like cabinbread
    Nephews like bananas.
And you could've packed us in
a big car, a big house, the best school
a marriage that would've worked like the best
the most American helicopter in the world.

James K. Baxter

Charm for Hilary

May the Pleiads seven
And the powers of Heaven
Keep thee night and day
From harm and disarray.
In thy body neither
Cough, nor colic either;
Fume of woodsmoke leave thee
Whole; nor chill wind grieve thee.
Spider black and hairy
Nowhere lurk to scare thee,
Whining midge to bother,
Prowling cat to smother.
Lie on pillows white
Through the rainy night;
No opossum leaping
Stir thee from thy sleeping,
Nor the mouse's laughter
Chittering on the rafter.
And ever, while thou
Like young wood dost grow –
By thy bed and board,
Hand on burning sword
Holy Michael guard thee,
From ill demons ward thee.

Alistair Te Ariki Campbell

Friend:

This is the dearest of my wishes,
The last leaf shaken from the tree:
Sow the southerly with my ashes
To fall in tears on Kapiti.

Janet Charman

the present table

his letter read
he had to marry
another girl
who was in trouble
our wedding was
off
they pulled down the marquee
in the garden
and folded the trestles
while i packed up the present table
but Aunt said
i was to keep her gift
you can always do
with an embroidered cloth

so I wed your Father
in blue
and it suited me
too

Glenn Colquhoun

A spell to be used when addressing the birth of a child

Let your first breath be
the volume of small lemons.

Let your second breath snap
like a sail in strong wind.

Let your third breath howl like a wolf
on the edge of a great mountain.

Let your fourth breath
hoot like an owl.

Let your fifth breath open slowly
like the eye of a wild animal.

Let your sixth breath
rise like the sun.

Let your seventh breath follow
the tide on its way out.

Let your eighth breath
guide it back in.

Sam Hunt

My Father Scything

My father was sixty when I was born,
twice my mother's age. But he's never been
around very much, neither at the mast
round the world; nor when I wanted him most.
He was somewhere else, like in his upstairs
Dickens-like law office counting the stars;
or sometimes out with his scythe on Sunday
working the path through lupin toward the sea.

And the photograph album I bought myself
on leaving home, lies open on the shelf
at the one photograph I have of him,
my father scything. In the same album
beside him, one of my mother.
I stuck them there on the page together.

My Father Today

They buried him today
up Schnapper Rock Road,
my father in cold clay.

A heavy south wind towed
the drape of light away.
Friends, men met on the road,

stood round in that dumb way
men stand when lost for words.
There was nothing to say.

I heard the bitchy chords
of magpies in an old-man
pine . . . *My* old man, he's worlds

away – call it Heaven –
no man so elegantly
dressed. His last afternoon,

staring out to sea,
he nods off in his chair.
He wonders what the

yelling's all about up there.
They just about explode!
And now, these magpies here

up Schnapper Rock Road . . .
They buried him in clay.
He was a heavy load,

my dead father today.

Anna Jackson

Catullus for babies

Look at you, balled up
asleep like the sun.

You have lived your whole life.
You have hardly begun.

You rise up
not just in the mornings

but again and again
through the night —

a sun out of sync,
a mad dawn that repeats

days running up
and over the screen

like a TV with the tracking
on the blink —

How many sleeps
till the morning?

Let's roll it all up
into one.

Johnny's minute

You promise to have your bath in a minute.

Not now, because now
you are glueing a beach,
you are painting the sky,
and fixing three beasts
so they'll stand
upright
on paper legs.

You don't need a minute,
you need a life time.

I'll have run a bath
as full as the Pacific Ocean,
warmed your pyjamas
up to the heat
of the core of the earth,
and swept up
enough grains of dust
to make a new planet out of

by the time your world is ready for me.

Cilla McQueen

Joanna

I visit my friend's kitchen.
There are roses on the floor

and a table with pears.
Her face is bare in the light.

She smiles. She has hung
a curtain. I like the darkness

inside our Dunedin houses
even in summer, the doors

that open into the hall, the
front door that opens into the sun.

Fardowsa Mohamed

Tuesday

the sun through the kitchen windows carpeted the tiles
like orange prayer mats and my mother was singing the folk song
I had memorised without understanding. steam rose from the stove
and condensed on the discoloured ceiling as she baked canjeero.
I ate five to impress my father, who told me to eat so that you are strong,
eat to feed your power. and I believed him, even if just for the morning
before the world rose against me. my mother hurried me into the car
as I nervously tugged at my strange clothes, picking out the ugly
before others did it for me. she held my chin up with her thumb and said:
*It is only Tuesday, macaanto. The week is young and the days have not
yet worn her down.*

Gregory O'Brien

The Location of the Least Person

Today went looking
for the least person
    among Japanese screens
and the playful volcanoes
           clouds trip over

among the jostling constellations
while critics dozed inside
    their cosy ruins
elbows resting on the foggy
librarians of this unwritten
          unspoken sorrow. Today
went looking for the least person

peeled an over-ripe orange
then swallowed
    the reflection
of a diver in a pool
only to realise all piano thieves
were in fact paradise swans

      only to find
the least person asleep in its lap
wearing massive shoes
    on his pin-sized feet
feeling tiny but growing
        incredibly larger.

Roma Potiki
(Te Rarawa, Te Aupōuri, Ngāti Rangitihi)

Big Susanah

Big Susanah rides past on a bicycle
man, her dreadlocks are swinging.

She's got a mean smile
and eyebrows to match.
Her cherry-toothed boots
can foot it anywhere.

Big Susanah
had eggs for breakfast
two and sunny-side up.

She's like a fast American,
English street-kid in Puerto Rico
got post-punk blues,
extra-terrestrial feminist with the
side of the head shaved like a
little girl lost
woman.

And when she smiles
you remember . . .

She isn't a
deep south blues mama,
she's your cousin
from Lower Hutt,
remember.

Jessie Puru
(Ngāti Te Ata, Tainui, Ngāpuhi)

Whāngai

Koro picked him up from the office they moved him to
still wet from the womb
sucking on his tongue waiting for mīraka,
mother still being stitched and sedated.

Koro wanted to slap
the social worker's hand away from him
he took him back to the whare
in the night

His body was always slick
like he'd just emerged from an ocean.

They often found him paddling
or fending off creatures in his sleep

As an adolescent
his obsession for catching the biggest creature
from Tangaroa's depths
grew bigger

'Careful out there' Koro would say
while his body blurred just past his vision
out the back door.

He'd pause, and lean up to face Koro
'You know I will be'
and held his aged face between his hands
before taking off again.

Robert Sullivan
(Ngāpuhi, Kāi Tahu, Irish)

Voice carried my family, their names and stories

Their names and fates were spoken.
The lands and seas of the voyage were spoken.
Calls of the stroke at times were spoken.
Celestial guidance, sightings, were spoken.
Prescriptions – medical and spiritual – were spoken.
Transactions – physical and emotional – were spoken.
Family (of), leaders (to), arguments, were well spoken.
Elders (of), were well spoken.
Burials were spoken.
Welcomes at times were spoken.
Futures lined up by pasts, were spoken.
Repeating the spoken were spoken.
Inheritance, inheritors, were spoken.
Tears at times were spoken.
Representations at first were spoken.
The narrator wrote the spoken.
The readers saw the spoken!
Spoken became unspoken.
[Written froze spoken.]

Albert Wendt

Son

Son, come let's build a house of good dreams
in our hearts
and clear a bright path to it
through flame trees
as healing as your mother's smile.
And when I die you can walk
the path to that house
and find me sitting
at my desk writing
this poem.

The wind that blows today
from Nukulau Island smells
of fierce wood fires
and feels like dry ash
on my skin.

Haare Williams

(Te Aitanga a Māhaki, Rongowhakaata, Tūhoe)

Koroua

E Koro – kaua e haere
Don't leave
who will make
fresh footprints
tracing our own
in the sand

E Koro – kaua e haere
Don't leave
who will kindle
the fires
smoke
to tease the nostrils

E Koro – kaua e haere
Don't leave
who will sing the melody
from beyond the shore
to linger
in the corridors of the mind

E Koro – kaua e haere
Don't leave
who will growl
when we're out of tune
so that music flows
from broken guitar strings

E Koro – kaua e haere
Don't leave
who will paddle us
through the misty
drift of
inconsequential tides

E Koro – kaua e haere
Auē taukiri ē
E Koro
Don't leave

Ashleigh Young

Triolet with Baby

(after 'Triolet with Pachyderm' by Hailey Leithhauser)

You don't have to have the baby right now
you just have to decide whether someday you will.
You don't have to hold the baby high above a pressing
    crowd
don't have to sprint to the boatyard and row
through a hurricane with the baby. You don't have to
    throw
yourself between an angry elephant seal and the baby.
    A black-backed gull
hasn't carried the baby away. You don't have to have the
    baby now,
you only have to decide whether someday you will.

Histories, Stories

Johanna Aitchison

Miss Dust loses her key

Hands and knees, digging
into the secret spot

in the garden of her half-
house. There's no dirt

that could be blacker
than her heart: a balloon

she insists on blowing
to full capacity, to float

off across the bitumen,
to be lit up by wise

lamp posts, which hang
their steel necks,

delicate as swans,
making their elegant way

across a lake in a place
which is not this place.

James K. Baxter

Lament for Barney Flanagan
(Licensee of the Hesperus Hotel)

Flanagan got up on a Saturday morning,
Pulled on his pants while the coffee was warming;
He didn't remember the doctor's warning,
  'Your heart's too big, Mr Flanagan.'

Barney Flanagan, sprung like a frog
From a wet root in an Irish bog –
May his soul escape from the tooth of the dog!
  God have mercy on Flanagan.

Barney Flanagan R. I. P.
Rode to his grave on Hennessy's
Like a bottle-cork boat in the Irish Sea.
  The bell-boy rings for Flanagan.

Barney Flanagan, ripe for a coffin,
Eighteen stone and brandy-rotten,
Patted the housemaid's velvet bottom –
  'Oh, is it you, Mr Flanagan?'

The sky was bright as a new milk token.
Bill the Bookie and Shellshock Hogan
Waited outside for the pub to open –
  'Good day, Mr Flanagan.'

At noon he was drinking in the lounge bar corner
With a sergeant of police and a racehorse owner
When the Angel of Death looked over his shoulder –
  'Could you spare a moment, Flanagan?'

Oh the deck was cut; the bets were laid;
But the very last card that Barney played
Was the Deadman's Trump, the bullet of Spades –
  'Would you like more air, Mr Flanagan?'

The priest came running but the priest came late
For Barney was banging at the Pearly Gate.
St Peter said, 'Quiet! You'll have to wait
  For a hundred masses, Flanagan.'

The regular boys and the loud accountants
Left their nips and their seven-ounces
As chickens fly when the buzzard pounces –
  'Have you heard about old Flanagan?'

Cold in the parlour Flanagan lay
Like a bride at the end of her marriage day.
The Waterside Workers' Band will play
  A brass goodbye to Flanagan.

While publicans drink their profits still,
While lawyers flock to be in at the kill,
While Aussie barmen milk the till
  We will remember Flanagan.

For Barney had a send-off and no mistake.
He died like a man for his country's sake;
And the Governor-General came to his wake.
  Drink again to Flanagan!

Despise not, O Lord, the work of Thine own hands
and let light perpetual shine upon him.

Ben Brown

(Ngāti Paoa, Ngāti Mahuta)

The Brother come home

(for Chris Campbell)

The Brother come home from the city
He done with the concrete cold
Steel heart got him angry
All that Babylon burned him out

The Brother come home from the city
Walked the holy road to the eastern shore
Washed himself salt clean
Smoked his sacrament in the company
of acolytes

The Brother come home from the city
Built him a whare high up on a hill
Tilled him a garden
Scattered his seeds
Carried his water
Reaped in the season

The Brother come home from the city
Blood him a tribe for his troubles
Run with the horsemen riding hard
through his sorrows
Scorning his fate

The Brother come home from the city
Torched the master's house
Cut down his neighbour's fences
Vindication in the Book
Leviticus lit and Moses burned
the damned thing to the ground

The Brother come home from the city
Walked the one-way road man
Don't we all
To the grim gate
Baring heart and soul
To the neighbour's rage
And the master's will
They shot him down

The Brother came home from the city
And home he stayed.

True hori story

Hori plays bass
He got no guitar case for
his instrument
Always leaves it behind
at gigs
Rings up the cuz
in the morning
'You got my bass bro?'
'I dunno, I'll go have a look'
Bass always makes it home
Just like greenstone
Hori sits on a groove tight as
Ain't no show pony though
Too cool for that
He got two eyes like most of us
One stares right through you
The other looks at heaven
Can be disconcerting

Janet Charman

From high days and holy days

8. Anzac Day

dusted with poppy
these biscuits
to help you forget

Allen Curnow

House and Land

Wasn't this the site, asked the historian,
Of the original homestead?
Couldn't tell you, said the cowman;
I just live here, he said,
Working for old Miss Wilson
Since the old man's been dead.

Moping under the bluegums
The dog trailed his chain
From the privy as far as the fowlhouse
And back to the privy again,
Feeling the stagnant afternoon
Quicken with the smell of rain.

There sat old Miss Wilson,
With her pictures on the wall,
The baronet uncle, mother's side,
And the one she called The Hall;
Taking tea from a silver pot
For fear the house might fall.

People in the *colonies*, she said,
Can't quite understand . . .
Why, from Waiau to the mountains
It was all father's land.

She's all of eighty said the cowman,
Down at the milking-shed.
I'm leaving here next winter.
Too bloody quiet, he said.

The spirit of exile, wrote the historian,
Is strong in the people still.
He reminds me rather, said Miss Wilson,
Of Harriet's youngest, Will.

The cowman, home from the shed, went drinking
With the rabbiter home from the hill.

The sensitive nor'west afternoon
Collapsed, and the rain came;
The dog crept into his barrel
Looking lost and lame.
But you can't attribute to either
Awareness of what great gloom
Stands in a land of settlers
With never a soul at home.

The Skeleton of the Great Moa in the Canterbury Museum, Christchurch

The skeleton of the moa on iron crutches
Broods over no great waste; a private swamp
Was where this tree grew feathers once, that hatches
Its dusty clutch, and guards them from the damp.

Interesting failure to adapt on islands,
Taller but not more fallen than I, who come
Bone to his bone, peculiarly New Zealand's.
The eyes of children flicker round this tomb

Under the skylights, wonder at the huge egg
Found in a thousand pieces, pieced together
But with less patience than the bones that dug
In time deep shelter against ocean weather:

Not I, some child, born in a marvellous year,
Will learn the trick of standing upright here.

Ruth Dallas

Tinker, Tailor

Tinker, tailor, who can show,
Who that passes can discover
Of old men seated in a row
Which was the deserted lover,
Soldier, sailor, who can tell
Hero now from ne'er-do-well?

Sooner that young mother find
Who can in sun or firelight see
A man grown old and deaf or blind
In the child upon her knee.

Silk, satin, who can trace
In a slow and heavy tread,
See in some old woman's face
The girl who danced the moon to bed,
Is there no one that can tell
Now the wallflower from the belle?

Find two lovers deep in grass
Who can see themselves grown old,
Summer into autumn pass,
And their love turn winter cold.

Murray Edmond

Mr Wat

washed my hair and cleaned my teeth
rinky-dinky world all right

returning to my wonky shack
kick my boots and hang my hat

bird outside on the wattle
first chants OM then drinks the bottle

choker wraps the skull from wind
Buddha in the pocket sings

c'est la vie Bohémienne
the old songs sound beyond belief

thunder by day ice by night
a cardboard box tied with string

that's where I keep everything

Fiona Farrell

Charlotte O'Neil's Song

You rang your bell and I answered.
I polished your parquet floor.
I scraped out your grate
and I washed your plate
and I scrubbed till my hands were raw.

You lay on a silken pillow.
I lay on an attic cot.
That's the way it should be, you said.
That's the poor girls' lot.
You dined at eight
and slept till late.
I emptied your chamber pot.
The rich man earns his castle, you said.
The poor deserve the gate.

But I'll never say 'sir'
or 'thank you ma'am'
and I'll never curtsey more.
You can bake your bread
and make your bed
and answer your own front door.

I've cleaned your plate
and I've cleaned your house
and I've cleaned the clothes you wore.
But now you're on your own, my dear.
I won't be there any more.
And I'll eat what I please
and I'll sleep where I please

and you can open your own front door.

Bernadette Hall

early settler

you dream a hand
   that will stitch a flag
to the bullet-hole
   in your shoulder

you dream a man
   who wears a huia feather,
stands all Heathcliff
   in the doorway
of the prefabricated house

you dream a door-post
   painted with your insignia:
a monkey, a black swan feather,
   a bike lock

Sam Hunt

We had a horse

1.

We had a horse, Phar Lap,
his stride, perfect as it gets.
As for me, it's the last lap –
a good gallop,
few worries, no regrets.

2.

We had a horse. He gave –
when times were merciless –
people reason to live.
He gave us punters hope;
more or less.

3.

We had a horse. And that,
for us,
mattered more than a house.
You can't ride a house
out of town.

Andrew Johnston

Hypermarket

The carparks divide
into continents;
the staff skate around, inside,
with hyperconfidence.

You go in looking
for a clock or a pear
and emerge, hours later,
with a deck chair;

as you cross the world
in search of the car
a fresh wind fills the canvas
somewhere off the coast of Africa.

Erik Kennedy

The Class Anxiety Country Song

I pull into the station,
tell them where I'm headed,
ask which has fewer calories,
diesel or unleaded.

I'm leaving behind a heartbreak,
a boy by the name of Regan.
I thought he was a Libra
and he thought honey was vegan.

I'm fixing to go up north,
where the stars are cold and quavery,
to a town with no pretentions
and a juice bar and a bakery,

and maybe I'll find love there.
I know that I'll be looking—
for a boy with cinnamon hair
who reads Murray Bookchin.

And if I don't come back
it's because I'm somewhere better,
with a boy and some land and a cat
and drugs and an Irish setter.

I 3D-printed a banjo
to play this scratchy song.
If the easy way is right,
then God, he made me wrong.

Bill Manhire

An Inspector Calls

We tiptoed into the house.
The neighbourhood was quiet as a mouse.

I felt very on edge. The money
was in the oven, not the fridge.

*

I glanced at the note on the piano.
Uh oh, uh oh, uh oh.

*

There's always a point at which a routine enquiry
turns into something else entirely.

I had to shoulder my way in.
The bathtub was simply full of the victim.

Ria Masae

Parousia

Jesus died this morning

in a nameless alleyway
hunched between an
ex-jailbird and a homeless girl.

I saw him last night
tickling the feet of fa'afafine
with his bearded kisses.

I heard him last night
laughing with hardened Magdalenas
over plastic cups of street brew.

I felt him last night
kiss cleansing across the depression
furrowed on my forehead.

You missed him –
the Second Coming has come and gone.

You were too preoccupied
scouring penthouse suites in trump hotels
singing psalms to abusers on podiums
tasting bleach from make-it-rain teeth
and stroking feathers of corrupt wings.

Did you not learn from his first visitation
that he would come as One
of the wandering and uncrowned?

Did you not learn from his first stopover
that sinner and saviour
walk shoeless side by side
along bleeding crossroads?

Jesus died this morning

in a nameless alleyway
beneath your feet
while your nose pointed to the skies.

Tuini Ngāwai

(Te Whānau-ā-Ruataupare, Ngāti Porou)

Ngā rongo

Ngā rongo o te pakanga nei
Ka kapakapa te manawa ē
Ka māharahara te tinana ē
Auē auē te aroha ē!
Ka raparapa noa ngā whakaaro
He aha i riri ai te ao katoa?
He nui rawa no te mātauranga!
Purari Hitara, tangata hao!
Ngā rongo o te pakanga ē
Ka kapakapa te manawa ē
Ka māharahara te tinana ē—
Auē auē te aroha ē!

Ka tangi wairua atu ahau
Ki a koutou rā e Te Hokowhitu
I roto i te kino o tēnei wā!
Kia kaha, kia kaha rā!
Ka raparapa noa ngā whakaaro
He aha i whakaheke toto ē?
Hei aha ma purari Hitara,
Ka tohetohe! Nō reira rā
Ka tangi wairua atu ahau
Ki a koutou rā e Te Hokowhitu
I roto i te kino o tēnei wā!
Kia kaha, kia kaha rā!

The news

[Translated by Te Kumeroa Ngoingoi Pēwhairangi]

The news of this war
Makes our hearts beat,
Our minds and bodies are confused.
Alas, alas, what sorrow!
We keep on wondering
Why the world is at war.
There are far too many smart people!
Bloody Hitler, that greedy man!
The news of this war
Makes our hearts beat,
Our minds and bodies are confused.
Alas, alas, what sorrow!

We cry in spirit
For you, the sons of Tu
In these terrible times.
Be strong, be strong!
We keep on wondering
Why there is this bloodshed.
And still bloody Hitler
Fights to the bitter end!
We cry in spirit
For you, the sons of Tu
In these terrible times.
Be strong, be strong!

Janet Newman

The shearer

arrives in a dented Datsun,
ties the portable unit to a post
with electric-blue baling twine,
bundles the ewe against her crotch.

The wool is grey and stuck with docks
but when she shears it falls away
like taking off a robe. Underneath
is cream that gilded in sun looks gold.

Her arms, varnished with lanolin,
shine as under lights. The ewe's skin
is pink and flushed. Graceful,
their limbs and torsos entwine

until the lulling background buzz
of the handpiece ends. She unbends
as from a bow, pitches the gear
in the car like sacks of wheat,

drives across the ruts, the only
remembrance of their fleeting dance
the golden fleece, froth of lace
and tulle, bobbing on the back seat.

Nina Mingya Powles

Last Eclipse
(after Annie Dillard)

She travelled alone / She crossed the mountains / She watched the landscape innocently / She supported her head on her fist / She felt strange birds in the trees / She touched an avalanche / She moved towards it / She waited without air / She sweated into the cold / She became volcanic / She heard the moon unhook from her teeth / She felt a piece of sun detach / She dissolved with blue light into orchards / She became a colour never seen / She flooded all the valleys / She sensed the last sane moment approaching

Jessie Puru
(Ngāti Te Ata, Tainui, Ngāpuhi)

Matariki

The time of breathing into clasped hands
hovering over a lighter to make a flame

not knowing
that an angry man threw his eyes into the night

the belly of his shattered father
weeping rain for separation of earth and sky

harvesting bitter grudges
from minds like hardened soil

packing up the wounds with mud and whiskey
and opening doors to wait

for those curious to know
how sky maps granted our existence

how the weight of earth
pushed against tongues of oars

and our tīpuna pushed back
and won.

Elizabeth Smither

Miriam's Wedding Dress

Walking about the house while flatmates slept
In her cut but not sewn wedding gown
Pinned at waist, shoulder and hem
With gaping wounds like St Sebastian
One girlfriend woke and saw her in the door
Practising her altar walk and screamed.

Is this the gown of after or before
The final state, like sloughing off a skin
The ultimate dress to undress in
She wears for pleasure now, half-pinned:
The image of herself she cannot see
But feels in waking up the dead?

Robert Sullivan

(Ngāpuhi, Kāi Tahu, Irish)

Waka 99

If waka could be resurrected
they wouldn't just come out
from museum doors smashing
glass cases revolving and sliding
doors on their exit

they wouldn't just come out
of mountains as if liquidified
from a frozen state
the resurrection wouldn't just
come about this way

the South Island turned to wood
waiting for the giant crew
of Māui and his brothers
bailers and anchors turned back
to what they were when they were strewn

about the country by Kupe
and his relations
the resurrection would happen
in the blood of the men and women
the boys and girls

who are blood relations
of the crews whose veins
touch the veins who touched the veins
of those who touched the veins
who touched the veins

who touched the veins
of the men and women from the time
of Kupe and before.
The resurrection will come
out of their blood.

Apirana Taylor

(Ngāti Porou, Te Whānau-ā-Apanui, Ngāti Ruanui)

poem for a princess

once from the chiefly line
from the seed of the rangatira

there grew the most beautiful flower in all of Waikato

her petals rivalled Tama-nui-te-ra in splendour

she hauled her tribe from the jaws of Hine-nui-te-po
she lived her life for her people, never for herself

therein lies her strength and beauty

on the banks of the Waikato River
all the taniwha call her name

Princess Te Puea, Te Puea Herangi

he piko he taniwha Waikato taniwha rau

Chris Tse

[On Sunday]

On Sunday

the good people go to church,
the roasts are carved

the children play in their gardens, warned
to stay away from *that street*

where they will catch
incurable diseases or disappear

into some Chinaman's shed
never to see daylight again, destined

to become an example
for other children.

On Sunday

Lionel Terry went hunting
for a Chinaman.

Tim Upperton

Space

The space between Earth and Mars
is the space between two worlds.
It is the space between two words.
Earth calls out to Mars, but Mars
slowly turns away.
Earth calls out again.
Hey Mars! But there is no one
on Mars to hear. Earth sends people
to Mars. When the people arrive
at the silent, empty world,
there is great excitement.
Earth calls out, Hey Mars!
Mars calls back, Hey Earth!
And each world is glad
to be less alone.

Richard von Sturmer

Monday 26 June

The woman from the Reject China Shop
smokes a mean cigarette.

I've lowered my eyes.
I'm feeling perverse.

Every other day is so unseasonable.

Cars slide in and out
of whatever lies
beyond the window.

People keep watching the sky,
but there's no rain.

A man in concrete boots
walks up the outside wall
of a wooden house.

And the sun sets
inside a parking meter.

David M'Kee Wright

Shearing's Coming

There's a sound of many voices in the camp and on the track.
And letters coming up in shoals to stations at the back;
And every boat that crosses from the sunny 'other side'
Is bringing waves of shearers for the swelling of the tide.

For the shearing's coming round, boys, the shearing's coming round,
And the stations of the mountains have begun to hear the sound.

They'll be talking up at Laghmor of the tallies that were shore,
And the man who broke the record is remembered at Benmore;
And the yarns of strikes and barneys will be told till all is blue,
And the ringers and the bosses will be passed in long review.

For the shearing's coming round, boys, the shearing's coming round,
And the stations of the mountains have begun to hear the sound.

The great Orari muster and the drafting of the men
Like a mob of ewes and wethers will be surely told again;
And a lot of heathen places that will rhyme with kangaroo
Will be named along with ringers and the things that they can do.

For the shearing's coming round, boys, the shearing's coming round,
And the stations of the mountains have begun to hear the sound.

At last the crowds will gather for the morning of the start,
And the slowest kind of jokers will be trying to look smart;
And a few will get the bullet, and high hopes will have a fall,
And the bloke that talks the loudest stands a show of looking small.

For the shearing's coming round, chaps, the shearing's coming round,
And the voices of the workers have begun to swell the sound.

Politics

Hana Pera Aoake

(Ngāti Hinerangi me Ngāti Raukawa, Ngāti Mahuta, Tainui-Waikato, Ngāti Waewae)

From Perhaps we should have stayed

PERHAPS WE SHOULD'VE STAYED.
SOMETIMES THE LONGING MIGHT KILL YOU.
OTHER TIMES IT MIGHT JUST BE THE EXHAUSTION.
IT'S GOOD TO BE YEARNING.
MAYBE YOU YEARN FOR SOMEONE OR MAYBE YOU
JUST YEARN FOR SOMETHING BETTER.
WATCHING BODIES FROM VERY FAR AWAY
THROUGH A SCREEN DOES NOT GIVE YOU A SENSE
OF WHO SOMEONE REALLY IS.
PERHAPS WE SHOULD'VE STAYED.
THE IDEA OF HAPPINESS IS JUST CAPITALISM.

Behrouz Boochani

The Black Kite
[Translated by Ali Parsaei and Janet Galbraith]

Over Manus Island,
a black kite flies.

A few youths –
still with energy
to bear the difficulties
of this prison camp –
made it.

The black kite flies,
a messenger of freedom
for us, the forgotten prisoners.

It circles
higher and higher
above the camp,
above the beautiful coconuts.

Our eyes follow its flight,
it seems to want to tear its rope.

It breaks free,
dances towards the ocean,
flies far and again farther
until no one can see it.

The youths stare into the empty sky
after their impossible dream.

Jacq Carter
(Ngāti Awa, Ngāi Te Rangi, English, Irish)

Aroha

I gave to you a rock
from which you built a wall
then you stood there at the top
making me feel small

I gave to you a seed
from which you grew a tree
then you told me all its fruit
did not belong to me

kss kss auē hā

I took you to a mountain
you did not want to climb
instead you tunnelled deep inside
for treasures that were mine

I led you to the ocean
and taught you about the tides
now I go down to the shore
and all the fish have died

kss kss auē hā

I told you all my stories
you wrote down every word
now I find my stories
are no longer to be heard

I carved a piece of greenstone
and hung it round your neck
then you made a thousand more
only yours were made of plastic

kss kss auē hā

I gave birth to a daughter
a child for you and me
but you did all the parenting
so she wouldn't turn out like me

Then I signed your piece of paper
some kind of guarantee
that while you would watch over them
these things belonged to me

kss kss auē hā

I gave to you kāwanatanga
a kind of governing
but I didn't give you mana
because there's mana in being me

I embrace my own uniqueness
my rangatiratanga too
I will have the rights that you have
without having to be like you

kss kss auē hā

And one day I will walk again
the lands you stole from me
only this time I'll be standing tall
and Papatūānuku will be free

Janet Charman

the lecture on Judy Grahn

the wimmin carried in their ironing boards
set them up

plugged in their irons

they began ironing together   set on silk
raised it to linen
men's shirts   a few synthetics suffered

one of the wimmin
walked around the room
removing the asbestos pads
where the iron rests were   on old model boards
        (dangerous if cut or sawn)

when the shirts were ironed
the wimmin put them on
rolled the sleeves to the elbow
and drove home together
fast

they were not stopped

David Eggleton

My Inner Aotearoa

My inner Aotearoa is smoky blue gums
in a corner of the khaki paddock,
a crunching noise underfoot from withered grasses,
    the tarred road bleeding in the sun,
    creek beds shoaling as a dusty river,
    bush decked with trails of clematis flowers.
When I only had gorse in my pockets,
I went in fear of the spiralling arms
of Crab Nebula, somewhere overhead.
Now I escape to stamp the black bubbles
of hot bitumen as if treading grapes,
and run headlong up Breakneck Road.

My inner Aotearoa is a need to brake
to descend the incline,
and I want it steep, steeper, steepest.
    A riddled leaf smites my wet cheek,
    a hailstorm of lies
    is illuminated in a lightning flash.
A glacier shrinks to the size of an ice-cube,
to be crunched, steadily.
But dig deep, deeper, deepest,
throw up topsoil till it rains sustenance.
The magnitude of the extra grunt
resounds, as one more raindrop falls.

My inner Aotearoa is a lake's rise
and fall, land's a heartbeat.
The transcendental meaning of flesh
is raised on a bier,

> on a balsawood cross,
> on a barbecue grill,
> on a hospital bed.

Light thickens and sours in the milk bottle,
glugs heavily in the sinkhole,
leading to the place where all sinkholes empty.
So just hold your nose and jump,
into eternal darkness made visible.

Pictures of Home

Geothermal rock and roll never grows old,
there is a Price Freeze that never grows cold.
A mountain of sheep skulls, supermarkets in chains,
the blue vinyl paddling pool is full of rain.
Hedge trimmer, fruit juicer, a shapely finger,
say cheese, think butter, think milk, think bigger.
A bargain-basement black market
wool roots anger in the shagpile carpet.
Patchouli clouds, the smell of rubbish also rises,
bleeding fairies in a gone-wrong fairy-tale crisis.
Smorgasbord spread across the Dairy Board,
Anchor Butter autographed by Samuel Butler.
Hacking at the frozen meat,
kākāpō going cheap.
New Zealand, who? Somebody's baby turning blue.
New Zealand, where?
A Social Welfare questionnaire.
New Zealand, where?
The stuffing knocked out of a teddy bear.
On the colour TV in the Lebanese Takeaways,
the Thing is running Round the Bays.

Prime Time

The sun loves hot February to death,
girls do the hula till they're out of breath.
Youths on beaches are flinging Frisbees.
Chaps in board shorts strut the Bee's Knees.
A tiara of lights on the Harbour Bridge,
a Cockroach Democracy behind the fridge.

Gross Crazies of the Junkosphere
are doing the backstroke through their beer.
Spiderman dangles from the lampshade,
a plastic goldfish swims in lemonade.
Civilisation smoked down to the filtertip.
Jehovah in a cloudburst would mean abandon ship.
Coronary bypass drunks pilot cannibal cars,
pursuing their own Paradises, Xanadus, Shangri-Las.

A. R. D. Fairburn

In the Younger Land

This stubborn beach, whereon are tossed
white roses from the sea's green bough,
has never sheathed a Norman prow
nor flinched beneath a Roman host;

yet in my bones I feel the stir
of ancient wrongs and vanished woes,
and through my troubled spirit goes
the shadow of an old despair.

Fiona Farrell

The thread

She wipes her hands of all that.
No more cakes and bread.
No one to be cared for.
No one to be fed.

She puts on her dancing dress,
silver sandals on her feet.
But still she turns at any child
who calls on any street

'Mu-um! Mu-um!'

The fledgling call.
Lamb's bleat.

She stops and turns her head.

Her fine free silver dancing feet
caught by a dangling thread.

Gregory Kan

[There's a room]

There's a room

that we keep finding ourselves in

and in that room

there's a river

and in that river

there's a voice

and in that voice

there's a history of power

that we eat in black mouthfuls

barely coming up for breath.

Anne Kennedy

I was a feminist in the eighties

To be a feminist you need to have
a good night's sleep.

To be a feminist you need to
have your consciousness raised
and have a good night's sleep.

To be a feminist you need to
have regard for your personal well-being
have your consciousness raised
and have a good night's sleep.

To be a feminist you need to
have a crack at financial independence
have regard for your personal well-being
have your consciousness raised
and have a good night's sleep.

To be a feminist you need to
champion women, have a crack at
financial independence, have regard
for your personal well-being
have your consciousness raised and
have a good night's sleep.

To be a feminist you need to do the
childminding, washing, shopping, cooking and cleaning
while your mind is on higher matters
and champion women, have a crack
at financial independence, have regard
for your personal well-being
have your consciousness raised

and have a good
night's sleep.

To be a feminist you need to button
your coat thoughtfully, do the childminding
washing, shopping, cooking and cleaning
while your mind is on higher matters
and champion women, have a crack at
financial independence, have regard for
your personal well-being, have your
consciousness raised and have
a good night's
sleep.

To be a feminist you need to
engage in mature dialogue with
your spouse on matters of domestic
equality, button your coat thoughtfully
do the childminding, washing, shopping, cooking and cleaning
while your mind is on higher matters
and champion women, have a crack at
financial independence, have regard
for your personal well-being, have
your consciousness raised and
have a good
night's
sleep.

Then a lion came prowling out of the jungle
and ate the feminist all up.

These Scholars at the Picnic One Day

My poem about the hot day Susan and I

lunched by the river might be boring with just

us in it so I'll add a man, a scholar I think

and give him an elbow to lean on while talking

to my other invention, the other scholar

who'll be nutting out an ontological problem

and so gazing upwards glassily and of course

nestled up to me. But here's the thing,

just for a laugh I'll dress these scholars.

Yes, I'll give them black serge jackets

although it's like 30 degrees, grey flannel

trousers, thick shirts and cravats. Hey,

and a fez each, not to be pretentious

but they'll look a little pretentious

and perhaps even be a little and Susan

will go to swim half-dressed in the river.

I'll be a bit pissed at her for ditching me

and truth be told self-conscious at being left

the only normal one on the grass. In the

struggle to dress the men we've spilled

the picnic in the leaves so there's no food.

Eventually I'll realise that the first scholar

is not talking to the other scholar but to me

expounding on the nature of art. I will find

it boring and will be sorry I ever thought

to add these men to the lunch on the grass.

I will look away, I'll look, reader, at you

hoping you'll interpret my pleading expression,

take off your clothes and drop them one by one

on the grass as you come over

to rescue me.

Rachel McAlpine

From **Somewhere a Cleaner**

7.

Somewhere a poet
is cleaning a bathroom.
Somewhere a cleaner
is writing a poem.

Cilla McQueen

Timepiece

I got home from work & looked at
my watch, & it said
Ten to five, so I did the washing &
picked some greens & tidied up the
kitchen, & sat down & had a cup of coffee,
& looked at my watch & still it said
Ten to five, so I did some ironing &
made the beds & thought Hell I might
get all the housework done in one day
for a change, then looked at my watch
but nope, no change, & I turned on the
radio & it said Ten to five, so
I cleaned the bathroom like mad &
picked some flowers & wrote some
letters & some cheques & scrubbed
the kitchen floor & got started on the
windows – by this time I was getting a bit
desperate I can tell you, I was thinking
alternately Yay! soon there'll be no more to
do & I'll be free, & Jeez what if I
RUN OUT? I did in fact run out, & out,
& out, past the church clock saying
Ten to five & the cat on the corner with
big green eyes ticking away, & up into the
sky past the telephone wires, &
up into the blue, watchless, matchless, timeless
cloud-curtains, where I hide, &
it is silent, silent.

Selina Tusitala Marsh

Calabash Breakers

we all know
the calabash breakers
the hinemoas
the mauis
the younger brother
the only sister
the orphan
the bastard child
with rebellious blood

we all know
the hierarchies
the tapu
the boundaries
always crossed
by someone
petulant

we all know
the unsettled
the trouble makers
the calabash breakers
they sail the notes of our songs
stroke the lines of our stories
and reign in the dark hour

we should know them
we now need them
to catch bigger suns

Courtney Sina Meredith

Brown girls in bright red lipstick

have you seen them
with their nice white boyfriends
paisley scarves on scarred shoulders
looking for their wings

Brown girls in bright red lipstick
where the hell are they it's Sunday
driving 80s commodores
knees dangling kitchen benches

Brown girls in bright red lipstick
have you seen them
with their nice white girlfriends
reading Pablo Neruda
on fire the crotch of suburbia

What's inside her
fingers Jesus penis
the old testament
she's promised to a Tongan welder
or a buff Cookie cliff diver

Brown girls in bright red lipstick
have you seen them at the beaches
drowned in virgin olive oil
twirling their hair into soil

Brown girls in bright red lipstick
rearranged up on the stage
making your soft brothers
run broken home to mother

have you seen them washed in twilight
struck by hours and the colours
running like mascara
taking yet another lover
she can't sleep she's walking thunder

Brown girls in bright red lipstick
have you seen them in the kitchen
shucking mussels cutting chicken
egging on the lone horizon

her dark centipedes are hidden
Manu Sina's glittered lace
are they veins or blue pathways
led to reddest change.

J. C. Sturm
(Taranaki, Whakatōhea)

He waiata tenei mo Parihaka

Have you heard of Parihaka
Between
Maunga Taranaki
And the sea

Where Te Whiti o Rongomai
And Tohu Kakahi
Preached
Passive resistance, not war?

Have you heard of Parihaka
Where Taranaki iwi
Gathered
Seeking a way to keep their land?

Non-violence was their choice
Peace their aim
Raukura their badge
Ploughs their only weapons.

They pulled down fences
Pulled out pegs
Then ploughed whatever
The settlers claimed was theirs.

Have you heard of Parihaka's
Boys and girls
Waiting outside the gates
When the mounted soldiers came

To rape and murder
Pillage and burn
To take Te Whiti and Tohu away
With all the ploughmen

And ship them south
To build a causeway
Around Dunedin's
Wintry harbour?

Have you heard of Taranaki iwi
Denied a trial,
Chained like dogs
In sealed caves and tunnels?

Ngai Tahu smuggled
Food and blankets
To the prisoners
Comforted the sick in the dark.

Kua ngaro nga tangata
Kua ngaro i te po!
Aue te mamae
That followed after!

If you haven't heard of Parihaka,
Be sure
Your grandchildren will
And their children after them,

History will see to that.
But for now,
He waiata tenei mo Parihaka —
Aue, aue, a-u-e —

Robert Sullivan
(Ngāpuhi, Kāi Tahu, Irish)

Old Government House

I want to wrap Old Government House
like Christo and Jean-Claude
I want to wrap Old Govt House
in pages of the Treaty
I want to wrap OGH
in lavalavas
I want to wrap OGH
in fine feather cloaks
I want to wrap OGH
in tartans
I want to wrap OGH
in parachute silk in balloon rubber
I want to wrap OGH
in illuminated vellum
I want to wrap OGH
in four enormous kanji blankets
for the north wind
for the south east and west winds
I want to rap its doors and say open sesame
so I did

Leilani Tamu

How to Make a Colonial Cake

i.

Take one wily whaler
(harpoons and fish hooks
burly men, rough and rugged
seasoned sailors
in love with the sea)

Add three bloody beachcombers
(shipwrecked and lost
afraid and alone
adopted   eaten   assimilated)

Mix in five tricky traders
(crooked and cut-throat
sex on a stick 'native' wives in tow
going troppo
in the fecund heat)

Stir in seven meddling missionaries
(chaste and two-faced
bibles loaded
ready to attack
Tagaloa's heartland)

ii.

Bake for 200 years at 38°C
(cut across
beaches and cultural
boundaries   protocols   languages   gene pools

as though the world was an oyster
a giant vagina
that only they could eat)

iii.

Ice with care: vanilla will displace chocolate
(as they succumbed to
enticement
excitement
addiction
affliction
horror

of the west)

iv.

Sprinkle with hundreds and thousands: indigenous variety
(sang   fought   laughed   cried
eventually
died)

Apirana Taylor
(Ngāti Porou, Te Whānau-ā-Apanui, Ngāti Ruanui)

Sad Joke on a Marae

Tihei Mauriora I called
Kupe Paikea Te Kooti
Rewi and Te Rauparaha.
I saw them
grim death and wooden ghosts
carved on the meeting house wall.

In the only Maori I knew
I called
Tihei Mauriora.
Above me the tekoteko raged.
He ripped his tongue from his mouth
and threw it at my feet.

Then I spoke.
My name is Tu the freezing worker.
Ngatai D.B. is my tribe.
The pub is my marae.
My fist is my taiaha.
Jail is my home.

Tihei Mauriora I cried.
They understood
the tekoteko and the ghosts
though I said nothing but
Tihei Mauriora
for that's all I knew.

Chris Tse

Super model minority – Reincarnations

I was a sky   when a sky meant untapped potential.

Now a sky   is the end of days—the unpredictable

nature of a world   melting and freezing at the same time.

I was a river   when a river meant speeding ahead

into the space   between new and remembered—always

a perilous chase.   Now a river is the earth turning against itself

in slow motion   a sick vein carrying needles to the brain.

I was a line   when a line was something you memorised.

Now a line   is what I bolt from with my flaming sword and shield

running blind   into a resolution that's been decided

for me. I had   an idea that would separate the heroes

from the thieves   but throwing my body against their walls

has taught me   a flag can't contain everything, but it says enough that

they raise their gun   whenever they see me approaching

Hone Tuwhare

(Ngāpuhi)

No Ordinary Sun

Tree let your arms fall:
raise them not sharply in supplication
to the bright enhaloed cloud.
Let your arms lack toughness and
resilience for this is no mere axe
to blunt, nor fire to smother.

Your sap shall not rise again
to the moon's pull.
No more incline a deferential head
to the wind's talk, or stir
to the tickle of coursing rain.

Your former shagginess shall not be
wreathed with the delightful flight
of birds nor shield
nor cool the ardour of unheeding
lovers from the monstrous sun.

Tree let your naked arms fall
nor extend vain entreaties to the radiant ball.
This is no gallant monsoon's flash,
no dashing trade wind's blast.
The fading green of your magic
emanations shall not make pure again
these polluted skies . . . for this
is no ordinary sun.

O tree
in the shadowless mountains
the white plains and
the drab sea floor
your end at last is written.

How to memorise and recite a poem

Zech Soakai: Verse, Vessel and Voice

I have been writing and performing poetry for just over ten years now, and the task of memorising poetry is one of the most arduous but rewarding parts of the creative process. There's something to be said about committing verse to memory, about vocalising each consonant and vowel through a lilt in the human voice, or through dedicating time to annotate poetry so that we might come to a deeper, more intimate understanding of the written word. It never gets easier, but it is always worth it. This is especially true when you have the added bonus of getting to share a poem with an audience. Suddenly, the labour of memorising the written word pays off in real time, as you're able to become a vessel for a poem to breathe and speak new life into others.

One of my favourite occasions of memorising and performing a poem is when I filmed the performance of my own poem 'Pink Plastic' for Tāmaki Paenga Hira, Auckland War Memorial Museum in 2012. Writing 'Pink Plastic' was in itself a spiritual experience. However, memorising and performing the beast was where the true challenge began. I say this because there is something incredibly rewarding about memorising a poem off by heart and then presenting it to others. If writing is the process of drawing within yourself to find poetic gold, then memorising and performing poetry is a way of releasing and sharing those gems, so that they might touch the hearts and minds of others.

Through my years of competing in poetry slams, and filming different projects, I have gathered a few tips and tricks to help with memorising and performing a poem, compiled here. Some of these tips are my own, and others are ones I have gained from valuable mentors on my artistic journey. You may also want to play around and see which strategies you can combine to help smooth out the memorisation process.

1. Write out your poem

With the increasing likelihood that most of our time spent with poetry is on some sort of digital device, when you're preparing to memorise and perform a poem, it is important to go back to basics and reach for the pen and paper, and physically write out your poem. Now I'm no neuroscientist, but I do know there is something that happens in the mind when we take time to write out a poem, as the act of writing on paper helps transfer lines of poetry into the body. Through writing out poems, we move poetry into the body, and when poetry sits in the body, it becomes easier to memorise, and in turn embody and perform. So write out the poem as many times as you need, and when it comes to the actual memorisation you will find it is a more manageable task.

2. Record yourself and listen to the playback

Poetry that is seen and heard on stage can feel like a great piece of music that continues to echo into our subconscious. This is a critical difference, and as Professor Selina Tusitala Marsh says, 'The difference makes the difference.' With this in mind, you want to always think about the aural and visual experience of a poem. To practise, read the poem aloud into a recording device, and then listen to its playback as you go about your life. The reason behind this strategy is three-fold. 1. You get to listen. You get to hear your voice, and become curious about the ways in which you can hone your voice to amplify the message of a poem. 2. You're listening to the poem constantly, so you're able to memorise it like you would your favourite song or rap. When I'm trying to memorise a poem, I've often found it useful to put the audio on repeat, and listen to it everywhere. Sometimes I will say the poem with my recorded voice, other times I will listen. Each time is an easy step towards knowing the poem more intimately. 3. This one relates back to number 1. You get to dig into the rhythmic possibilities of language. Listen, and I mean really listen, to each consonant. Get curious about how a line can change its meaning or tone when the stress is placed on different sounds or words within and across lines. Listening to a poem on repeat is a great way to break the monotonous surface of memorising a poem, and really find its essence. Once the spirit of a poem has presented itself to you, it becomes your duty to sharpen your biggest performance tools, i.e. the body and the voice, to amplify its essence.

3. Memorise your poem back to front

This is a strategy I was first introduced to by award-winning Australian poet Luka Lesson, during my time in Greece. The logic behind this strategy is to make sure you always finish strong. This is especially true if your purpose is to perform poetry to an audience. The idea is that if you memorise the last stanza first and so on, then regardless of how you start a poem, you'll always be able to rein it in, or shift to another level because the most comfortable parts of the poem happen to be the second half. Memorising your poem back to front is also a strategy you could adapt with recording yourself on a digital device and listening to the playback. The intention behind this strategy is that your performance gains momentum and confidence as you go through the poem. You never want to start a poem off strongly and then fade as you start to drop lines and miss key words. If you memorise a poem back to front, you'll find you have space and time to build into the poem, and that you will leave a lasting impression on an audience.

4. Beat the poem

Just like how a musician will have a score of music that has signs and symbols that show where dynamic changes are made, or where particular phrases are punctuated, performance poets will have a copy of their poem with scribbles between lines and along margins. This is what we refer to as beating the poem, and is especially important as you get closer to performing. With this strategy in mind, make sure you have a copy of your poem printed out and double spaced. From here, you want to put in any dynamic changes, or keywords/symbols that remind you to emote a specific emotion when you get to a particular line/phrase. I've also seen different poets highlight and colour code lines, depending on emotional intent and desired impact. Once you've broken the poem, you'll have yourself a little map of its emotional trajectory, and will know how to 'attack' the poem.

There are so many other strategies that you can use to effectively and efficiently memorise and perform a poem. However, I often come back to what my mentor and fellow poet Grace Taylor taught me: 'The stage is a privilege.' This philosophy has helped anchor me to the task of memorising and performing a poem as an act of commitment to craft and to audience. To memorise a poem is to take in all the words, thoughts and emotions in the poem. To perform/recite a poem is to channel all that energy for a concentrated moment, so that you might freeze time and allow others to be your world. Memorising and performing poetry is always a privilege. However, on its most powerful days it is also an opportunity for you to be a vessel for something greater, and for you to invite others into the world of the imagination. That is the power of poetry.

Rosalind Ali: On Teaching, Learning and Performing Poetry

As a high-school teacher of poetry over many years, I know that poems have special powers when read aloud. There is heightened awareness of music and rhythm and intricate connections between sound and sense in the language of poetry. Speaking poetry aloud is how we learn to know, to feel and to perform more effectively. A poem lives in our breath, our vocal chords, our diaphragm, our ears. To learn a poem by heart is to carry it with you, and to build reservoirs of story, language, knowledge and ideas. At the very least, encouraging us all to slow down as we journey through the reading of poems, to read closely and re-engage with the eye and the ear, may help us all feel and experience poems more deeply. Milan Kundera talks of 'a secret bond between slowness and memory, between speed and forgetting'. We need to nurture this bond.

Hearing poems aloud has resonated with many of us in our lives. For me, there was the fun in primary school, back in the day, of reciting Denis Glover's 'The Magpies' with its famous 'Quardle oodle ardle wardle doodle' onomatopoeic refrain. As a teacher, I have witnessed the impact of poets visiting the school: the voice and expression in Tusiata Avia's magnetic performance of 'My dog' to a captivated audience; the privilege of hearing Jenny Bornholdt's quiet reading of 'In the garden' and 'Instructions for how to get ahead of yourself while the light still shines'. These have been models for classroom experimentation with metaphor, pace, form – and importantly, with sound and performance.

Not all my students feel the same way about learning poems by heart. The phone's search and skim functions are so much faster and more reliable, they say. Why bother to memorise? But many are now discovering that engaging closely with a poem and committing it to memory can help them understand more acutely the voice, patterning, intricate connections and intriguing play of language that heighten emotional understanding and impact. And it's fun.

The poems in *Remember Me* remind us of the range of subjects, stories, styles and voices in New Zealand writing. Notice, for example, how repetition and sensory detail intensify mood in Hone Tuwhare's 'Rain', and formal metrical patterns and rhythms enhance his 'No Ordinary Sun'; how rhythm, rhyme and repetition in Glenn Colquhoun's sound-rich spell poems lend themselves to recitation and performance.

For teachers, this anthology offers valuable, thematically grouped material directly relevant to being a New Zealander. *Remember Me* offers significant range and diversity of New Zealand poems, poets, themes and forms to add to our teaching repertoire, as well as artistic models to inspire students in their own writing.

How do you learn a poem by heart and perform it?

Consider four key steps:

1. Explore

Browse the anthology. Read through slowly. Mark poems that resonate, that make an impression or arouse curiosity. Notice connections and patterns, forms and themes. Read/share a poem a day (at least). Build the reading and listening experience.

2. Understand the poem

Warm up: Choose a short poem or funny poem as a first step in modelling the memorisation process or to focus on an aspect of craft.

Use the following steps to model understanding and stages of learning the poems, as well as discussing how language, sound and structure contribute to meaning. I suggest the following poems as a start: 'Untitled' by J. C. Sturm, 'Consolation Prize' by Geoff Cochrane, 'Haiku (1)' by Hone Tuwhare, 'A New Tune' by Kevin Ireland, 'the present table' by Janet Charman, 'High Country Weather' by James K. Baxter, 'Charm for the Winter Solstice' by Airini Beautrais,

'E noho rā' by Jacq Carter, 'The guest house' by Mohamed Hassan, 'Wai ora' by Keri-Anne Stephens, 'Koroua' by Haare Williams.

- Read the poem carefully and see what it is about.
- Read the poem out loud.
- Re-read slowly and with care. What is the role of the title? Who is speaking? To whom? Tone and tonal shifts? What is the situation and setting of the poem? What is the story here? What might be the poet's meaning or intention? Deeper issues? Tensions and shifts? Pay attention to form, enjambment, sound, rhythm and the way meaning may unfold over line breaks and stanzas. Write down your initial thoughts or questions.
- Copy out the poem. Annotate closely. Write all around the poem, anything you notice about the words on the page: title, layout, speaker, voice, mood, distinctive images and sound, punctuation, the stressed/unstressed words and syllables, patterns of sound and imagery, repetition, and anything else that's curious or interesting.
- Share with a friend. Discuss your poem.

3. Memorise the poem

- Read your poem as many times as you can.
- Now learn the poem line by line. Repeat and repeat the lines. If there are rhymes, relish them.
- Speak what you see on the page, simply and clearly. Know the story of the poem.
- Locate the sentence, the sense units and how they play on the page. Be aware of punctuation and line breaks; avoid an automatic pause at the end of every line.
- The more senses you can draw on during the learning of the poem, the more effective your memorisation will be. Say and hear the words. Visualise the imagery. Draw the pictures. Write down the words by hand and be conscious of how the story, tensions or argument of the poem evolves. Try reading a line or two lines at a time and keep repeating them until they are part of you. Consider the tonal shifts. Explore rhythm and pace.

- Perhaps move around where you can walk and talk the lines.
- Keep the poem in your pocket, on your phone. Connect. It will become a special friend and companion. Many special friends.

Now, choose a longer poem you'd be happy to spend time with or that speaks to you. Repeat this process and move on to performance.

4. Perform the poem

What makes a compelling performance? Consider these tips to help draw the listener into the language, feeling and experience of the poem and your distinctive personal engagement.

- Show evidence of understanding: Work through the process above, making sure you know, feel and understand the poem fully. Be attentive to meanings, messages, tonal shifts, other nuances. Infuse the poem with your understanding and appreciation.
- Physical presence: Stand up. Hold your space. Be present and comfortable in your body. Look up and look out confidently. This is yours.
- Voice and articulation: Speak up and speak out. Speak clearly. Watch pitch, pace, emphasis and pause. Take your time. Don't rush or mumble.
- Consider dramatic appropriateness: Avoid the dramatic performance. Overdoing vocal emphasis and gesture can distract from the lines and storytelling. Use simple gestures as appropriate.

Finally and importantly, trust the writer.

Let the words do the work.

Relax and enjoy. You are ready to perform and share.

Go on.

Contributors and Sources

FLEUR ADCOCK's poems are selected from *Collected Poems: Fleur Adcock* (VUP, 2019).

JOHANNA AITCHISON's poem is from *Miss Dust* (Seraph Press, 2015).

HANA PERA AOAKE (Ngāti Hinerangi me Ngāti Raukawa, Ngāti Mahuta, Tainui-Waikato, Ngāti Waewae): The verse selected is an excerpt from 'Perhaps we should have stayed' which appears in *A Bathful of Kawakawa and Hot Water* (Compound Press, 2020).

The poem by TE AWHINA RANGIMARIE ARAHANGA (Rapuwai, Waitaha, Ngāti Māmoe, Ngāi Tahu) is from *Darkness in Light* (Steele Roberts, 2014).

NICK ASCROFT's poem is from *From the Author of* (VUP, 2000).

TUSIATA AVIA's poems are selected from *Wild Dogs Under My Skirt* (VUP, 2004).

The poem by HINEMOANA BAKER (Ngāti Raukawa, Ngāti Toa Rangatira, Te Ātiawa, Ngāi Tahu, German, English) is from *Mātuhi | Needle* (VUP, 2004).

SERIE BARFORD's poem is from *Sleeping with Stones* (Anahera Press, 2021).

JAMES K. BAXTER's poems are selected from *James K. Baxter: Complete Poems*, edited by John Weir (THWUP, 2022).

AIRINI BEAUTRAIS' 'charms' are from *Western Line* (VUP, 2011).

URSULA BETHELL's poems are selected from *Collected Poems: Ursula Bethell*, edited by Vincent O'Sullivan (VUP, 2021).

HERA LINDSAY BIRD's poem is from *Pamper Me to Hell & Back: Laureate's Choice 2018*, chosen by Carol Ann Duffy (Smith|Doorstop Books, 2018).

PETER BLAND's poem is from his collection *Nowhere is Too Far Off* (Cuba Press, 2020).

The poem by ARAPERA HINEIRA BLANK (Ngāti Porou, Ngāti Kahungunu, Rongowhakaata, Te Aitanga a Māhaki) can be found in *Puna Wai Kōrero: An Anthology of Māori Poetry in English*, edited by Reina Whaitiri and Robert Sullivan (AUP, 2014).

BEHROUZ BOOCHANI's 'Forgive me my love' appeared on The Spinoff, 13 Dec 2019, https://thespinoff.co.nz/books/13-12-2019/the-friday-poem-forgive-*me-my-love-by-behrouz-boochani* and 'The Black Kite' in Pen International, 20 June 2019, www.pen-international.org/news/two-poems-by-behrouz-boochani.

JENNY BORNHOLDT's 'Instructions for how to get ahead of yourself while the light still shines' is from *Moving House* (1989), 'The ox climbed a fir tree' and 'Wedding song' are from *How We Met* (1995), and 'In the garden' is from *This Big Face* (1988), all published by VUP.

The poem by BUB BRIDGER (Ngāti Kahungunu, Irish, English) can be found in *Puna Wai Kōrero: An Anthology of Māori Poetry in English*, edited by Reina Whaitiri and Robert Sullivan (AUP, 2014).

SARAH BROOM's poem can be found in her second collection *Gleam* (AUP, 2013).

Poems by BEN BROWN (Ngāti Paoa, Ngāti Mahuta) are from *Between the Kindling and the Blaze* (Anahera Press, 2013).

ROBBIE BURNS: 'To Mary in Heaven' can be found at BBC (Arts): www.bbc.co.uk/arts/robertburns/works/to_mary_in_heaven. 'Ki a Meri i Te Rangi', a translation by Rēweti Kōhere, can be found at National Library of New Zealand – Papers Past: https://paperspast.natlib.govt.nz/periodicals/TOATAK19271001.2.8.

ALISTAIR TE ARIKI CAMPBELL: 'The Return' and 'Friend' are from *The Collected Poems of Alastair Te Ariki Campbell* (VUP, 2016). 'Roots' can be found in *Whetu Moana: Contemporary Polynesian Poems in English*, edited by Albert Wendt, Reina Whaitiri and Robert Sullivan (AUP, 2002).

JACQ CARTER (Ngāti Awa, Ngāi Te Rangi, English, Irish): 'E noho rā' can be found in *Puna Wai Kōrero: An Anthology of Māori Poetry in English*, edited by Reina Whaitiri and Robert Sullivan (AUP, 2014). 'Aroha' can be found in *Whetu Moana: Contemporary Polynesian Poems in English*, edited by Albert Wendt, Reina Whaitiri and Robert Sullivan (AUP, 2002).

JANET CHARMAN's 'the present table' is from *Snowing Down South* (AUP, 2002), 'Anzac Day' is from the sequence 'high days and holy days' in *The Pistils* (OUP, 2022), and 'the lecture on Judy Grahn' is from *2 Deaths in 1 Night* (New Women's Press, 1987).

CADENCE CHUNG's poem is from the collection *Anomalia* (We Are Babies, 2022).

GEOFF COCHRANE's 'Consolation Prize' is from *Acetylene* (VUP, 2001), 'Our City and Its Hills' is from *Wonky Optics* (VUP, 2015) and 'The Sea the Landsman Knows' is from *The Sea the Landsman Knows* (Brick Row, 1980).

Poems by GLENN COLQUHOUN are from *Playing God* (Steele Roberts, 2002).

MARY CRESSWELL's poem is from *Body Politic* (The Cuba Press, 2020).

ALLEN CURNOW's poems are selected from *Allen Curnow: Collected Poems*, edited by Elizabeth Caffin and Terry Sturm (AUP, 2017).

RUTH DALLAS's poems are selected from her *Collected Poems* (OUP, 2000).

EILEEN DUGGAN's poems are chosen from *Selected Poems: Eileen Duggan*, edited by Peter Whiteford (VUP, 2019).

MURRAY EDMOND's poem is from *Shaggy Magpie Songs* (AUP, 2015).

Poems by DAVID EGGLETON are selected from his *The Wilder Years: Selected Poems* (OUP, 2021).

A. R. D. FAIRBURN's poem can be found in *Short Poems of New Zealand*, edited by Jenny Bornholdt (VUP, 2018).

RANGI FAITH (Kāi Tahu, Ngāti Kahungunu): 'Unfinished Crossword' is from *Unfinished Crossword* (Hazard Press, 1990); 'Karakia to a Silent Island' can be found in *Whetu Moana: Contemporary Polynesian Poems in English*, edited by Albert Wendt, Reina Whaitiri and Robert Sullivan (AUP, 2002); 'Spring star' can be found in *Puna Wai Kōrero: An Anthology of Māori Poetry in English*, edited by Reina Whaitiri and Robert Sullivan (AUP, 2014).

FIONA FARRELL's 'Charlotte O'Neil's Song' is from the sequence 'Passengers' in *Cutting Out* (AUP, 1987); 'The thread' is from *Nouns, Verbs, Etc. (Selected Poems)* (OUP, 2020).

SIA FIGIEL's 'Songs of the fat brown woman' can be found in *Whetu Moana: Contemporary Polynesian Poems in English*, edited by Albert Wendt, Reina Whaitiri and Robert Sullivan (AUP, 2002).

DENIS GLOVER's poems are chosen from *Selected Poems: Denis Glover*, edited by Bill Manhire (VUP, 1995).

PAULA GREEN's poem is from *Making Lists for Frances Hodgkins* (AUP, 2007).

BERNADETTE HALL's 'Really & Truly' is from *The Lustre Jug* (2009), 'Living out here on the plains' is from *Life & Customs* (2013) and 'early settler' is from *The Merino Princess: Selected Poems* (2004), all published by VUP.

MOHAMED HASSAN's poem is from *National Anthem* (Dead Bird Books, 2020).

DINAH HAWKEN's 'Faith' and 'Drama' are from *Sea-light* (2021) and 'Pure Science' is from *One Shapely Thing* (2006), both published by VUP.

Poems by NICOLE TITIHUIA HAWKINS (Ngāti Kahungunu ki Te Wairoa, Ngāti Pāhauwera) are from *Whai* (We Are Babies, 2021).

JEFFREY PAPAROA HOLMAN's sonnet is from *The Late Great Blackball Bridge Sonnets* (Steele Roberts, 2004).

Poems by KERI HULME (Kāi Tahu, Ngāti Māmoe, Nordic, Celtic) are selected from *Strands* (AUP, 1992).

SAM HUNT's poems are chosen from his *Coming to It: Selected Poems* (Potton & Burton, 2018).

ROBIN HYDE's poem can be found in *The Penguin Book of New Zealand Verse*, edited by Ian Wedde and Harvey McQueen (Penguin, 1986).

KEVIN IRELAND's poems are chosen from his *Selected Poems 1963–2013* (Steele Roberts, 2013).

Poems by ANNA JACKSON are from her collection *Catullus for Children* (AUP, 2003).

ANDREW JOHNSTON's 'How to Fly' is from *Birds of Europe* (2000) and 'Hypermarket' is from *Sol* (2007), both published by VUP.

GREGORY KAN's poems are from *Under Glass* (AUP, 2019).

ANNE KENNEDY's 'I was a feminist in the eighties' is from *Sing-song* (2003) and 'These Scholars at the Picnic One Day' is from *The Sea Walks Into a Wall* (2021), both published by AUP.

ERIK KENNEDY's 'There's No Place Like the Internet in Springtime' is from *There's No Place Like the Internet in Springtime* (VUP, 2019) and 'The Class Anxiety Country Song' is from *Another Beautiful Day Indoors* (THWUP, 2022).

MICHELE LEGGOTT's 'what is' is from *As Far as I Can See* (1999) and 'wild light' is from *Milk & Honey* (2005), both published by AUP.

JIAQIAO LIU's 'to a future you' can be found in *A Clear Dawn: New Asian Voices from Aotearoa New Zealand*, edited by Paula Morris and Alison Wong (2021) and 'that hand is for holding' in *Out Here: An Anthology of Takatāpui and LGBTQIA+ Writers from Aotearoa*, edited by Chris Tse and Emma Barnes (2021), both published by AUP.

ANNA LIVESEY's poem is from *The Moonmen* (VUP, 2010).

RACHEL MCALPINE's poems can be found in her collection *How to be Old* (The Cuba Press, 2020) and in the anthology *Somewhere a Cleaner*, edited by Adrienne Jansen (Landing Press, 2020).

CILLA MCQUEEN's poems are taken from *Poeta: Selected and New Poems* (OUP, 2018).

BILL MANHIRE's 'Little Prayers' and 'Huia' are from *Wow* (2020). 'Kevin' and 'An Inspector Calls' are from *Lifted* (2005), both published by VUP.

SELINA TUSITALA MARSH's poem is from *Fast Talking PI* (AUP, 2009).

RIA MASAE's 'Parousia' can be found in *AUP New Poets* 7 (AUP, 2020).

COURTNEY SINA MEREDITH's poem is from *Brown Girls in Bright Red Lipstick* (Beatnik, 2012).

KARLO MILA's poem is from *Dream Fish Floating* (Huia, 2005).

FARDOWSA MOHAMED's poem can be found in *Poetry New Zealand Yearbook* 2020 (MUP).

JANET NEWMAN's 'The shearer' is from *Unseasoned Campaigner* (OUP, 2021).

JOHN NEWTON's 'Beetle' is from *The Caxton Press Anthology: New Zealand Poetry 1972–1986* (Caxton Press, 1987).

The poem by TUINI NGĀWAI (Te Whānau-ā-Ruataupare, Ngāti Porou) can be found in *The Penguin Book of New Zealand Verse*, edited by Ian Wedde and Harvey McQueen (Penguin, 1986).

GREGORY O'BRIEN's 'Song' is from *Man with a Child's Violin* (Caxton, 1990); 'A patriot of the time of day', 'A Visiting Card' and 'The Location of the Least Person' are from *Location of the Least Person* (AUP, 1987).

BOB ORR's 'Song to Chelsea Wharf' and 'Song to Rangitoto' are from *Calypso* (AUP, 2008).

VINCENT O'SULLIVAN's 'The sentiment of goodly things' is from *Being Here: Selected Poems* (VUP, 2015).

JOANNA MARGARET PAUL's poem is from her *Like Love Poems: Selected Poems* (VUP, 2006).

The poem by TE KUMEROA NGOINGOI PĒWHAIRANGI (Te Whānau-ā-Ruataupare, Ngāti Porou) can be found in *The Penguin Book of New Zealand Verse*, edited by Ian Wedde and Harvey McQueen (Penguin, 1986).

Poems by KIRI PIAHANA-WONG (Ngāti Ranginui, Chinese, English) are from *Night Swimming* (Anahera Press, 2013).

The poem by ROMA POTIKI (Te Rarawa, Te Aupōuri, Ngāti Rangitihi) is from *Shaking the Tree* (Steele Roberts, 1996).

NINA MINGYA POWLES's poem is from her debut collection *Magnolia* 木蘭 (Seraph Press, 2020).

JESSIE PURU (Ngāti Te Ata, Tainui, Ngāpuhi): 'Whāngai' can be found on The Spinoff, 21 September 2021: https://thespinoff.co.nz/books/ 17-09-2021/the-friday-poem-whangai-by-jessie-puru. 'Matariki' can be found in Poetry Foundation, February 2018: www.poetryfoundation.org/ poetrymagazine/poems/145465/matariki.

ESSA MAY RANAPIRI (Ngāti Raukawa, Te Arawa, Ngāti Pukeko, Clan Gunn): 'Have you gone out at night in your favourite dress and then felt like shit?' is from *Ransack* (VUP, 2019); 'Silence, Part 2' can be found in *Ko Aotearoa Tātou: We Are New Zealand*, edited by Michelle Elvy, Paula Morris and James Norcliffe (OUP, 2020).

HELEN RICKERBY's excerpt from 'Ban Zhao' is taken from her collection *How to Live* (AUP, 2019).

ELIZABETH SMITHER's poems are chosen from *The Tudor Style: Poems New and Selected* (AUP, 1993).

The poem by RUBY SOLLY (Kāi Tahu, Waitaha, Kāti Māmoe) is from *Tōku Pāpā* (VUP, 2021).

The poem by KERI-ANNE STEPHENS (Ngāti Kahungunu) can be found in the anthology *Somewhere a Cleaner*, edited by Adrienne Jansen (Landing Press, 2020).

MICHAEL STEVEN's 'After Trakl' is from *The Lifers* (OUP, 2020).

J. C. STURM (Taranaki, Whakatōhea): 'Untitled' and 'He waiata tenei mo Parihaka' are from *Dedications* (1996), and 'Let go, unlearn, give back' is from *Postscripts* (2000), both published by Steele Roberts.

ROBERT SULLIVAN (Ngāpuhi, Kāi Tahu, Irish): 'Karakia Whakakapi' and 'Old Government House' are from *Tūnui | Comet* (2022), with the translation of 'Karakia Whakakapi' from *Pike Ake* (1993); 'Voice carried my family, their names and stories' is from *Voice Carried My Family* (2005); and 'Waka 99' is from *Star Waka* (1999), all published by AUP. 'Arohanui' is from *Shout Ha! to the Sky* (Salt Publishing, 2010).

LEILANI TAMU's poem is from *The Art of Excavation* (Anahera Press, 2014).

Poems by APIRANA TAYLOR (Ngāti Porou, Te Whānau-ā-Apanui, Ngāti Ruanui) are chosen from his *A Canoe in Midstream: Poems New & Old* (CUP, 2009).

The poem by TAYI TIBBLE (Te Whānau-ā-Apanui, Ngāti Porou) is from *Rangikura* (VUP, 2021).

The poem by ANTHONY TIPENE-MATUA is from the anthology, *Somewhere a Cleaner*, edited by Adrienne Jansen (Landing Press, 2020).

'Pōkarekare ana' is by PARAIRE HĒNARE TOMOANA (Ngāti Te Whatu-i-āpiti, Ngāti Kahungunu) and can be found along with its translation by Margaret Orbell in *The Penguin Book of New Zealand Verse*, edited by Ian Wedde and Harvey McQueen (Penguin, 1986).

CHRIS TSE's '[On Sunday]' is from *How to be Dead in a Year of Snakes* (2014) and 'Super model minority – Reincarnations' is from *Super Model Minority* (2022), both published by AUP.

Poems by BRIAN TURNER are chosen from his *Selected Poems* (VUP, 2019).

Poems by HONE TUWHARE (Ngāpuhi) are chosen from his *Small Holes in the Silence: Collected Works* (Vintage, 2016).

OSCAR UPPERTON's poem is from *New Transgender Blockbusters* (VUP, 2020).

TIM UPPERTON's poem is from *A Riderless Horse* (AUP, 2022).

RICHARD VON STURMER's 'Baso is Unwell' is from the sequence 'Blue Cliff Verses', and '[hey you sparrows!]' is from 'Sparrow Notebook', both of which appear in *Suchness: Zen Poetry and Prose* (HeadworX, 2005); 'Monday 26 June' is from the sequence 'Expresso Love Letters' which appears in *A Network of Dissolving Threads* (AUP, 1991).

The poem by ARIELLE WALKER (Taranaki, Ngāruahine, Ngāpuhi, Pākehā) can be found in *AUP New Poets 9* (AUP, 2023).

BRYAN WALPERT's poem is from *Native Bird* (Mākaro Press, 2015).

IAN WEDDE's 'Abat-jour' is from *Good Business* (2009); 'Shadow Stands Up' 6 and 18 are from the sequence of the same name that appears in *The Lifeguard* (2013), both published by AUP.

ALBERT WENDT's 'Son' is from *Shaman of Visions* (1984); 'In Your Enigma' is from *Photographs* (1995), both published by AUP.

'He Waiata Aroha' is from NGATI WHAKAHEMO and is taken from *Ngā Mōteatea: The Songs, Part One*, edited by Apirana Ngata and translated by Pei Te Hurinui Jones (AUP, 2004). The following notes accompany the text: 'Ko ngā kupu o te waiata nei he mea tango mai i te pukapuka a Elsdon Best, i tā Tiwana Turi hoki, ā e tukua atu ana ki te kimi i ōna tino whakamārama. Ko te āhua o te wāhi i whakakaupapatia ai tēnei waiata kei te taha tai i tua mai o Maketu, kei Pukehina. Ko Ngati Whakahemo te iwi kei reira; nā reira ka whakamau pērā te pātai. He waiata reka tēnei, kei ngā wāhi katoa e waiatatia ana. / The text of this song was taken from the collections by Elsdon Best and that of [Tiwana] Turi, and it is offered here as an invitation for some explanation of it. It would appear that the locality where it was composed is on the seaward side of Maketu, at Pukehina. Ngati Whakahemo is the tribe living there: wherefore, the quest for information is directed to that tribe. This song has a sweet air and it has a vogue throughout the land.'

The poem by HAARE WILLIAMS (Te Aitanga a Māhaki, Rongowhakaata, Tūhoe) can be found in *Puna Wai Kōrero: An Anthology of Māori Poetry in English*, edited by Reina Whaitiri and Robert Sullivan (AUP, 2014).

Poems by BRIAR WOOD (Ngāpuhi Nui Tonu) are from *Rāwāhi* (Anahera Press, 2017).

SUE WOOTTON's poems are from *Magnetic South* (Steele Roberts, 2008).

'Shearing's Coming' by DAVID M'KEE WRIGHT can be found on RootsWeb: https://sites.rootsweb.com/~nzlscant/shearers.htm#SHEARING.

ASHLEIGH YOUNG's poem is from *How I Get Ready* (VUP, 2019).

ROSALIND ALI has facilitated community writing classes for young people over many years, including at the Michael King Writers Centre Young Writers Programme where she edited the literary journal, *Signals*. She leads the Writing Programme at St Cuthbert's College.

ZECH SOAKAI is an award-winning performance poet of Tongan and Samoan descent with links to both Poutasi, Upolu, Samoa, and Ha'ato'u, Pangai, Ha'apai.

Thanks

My heartfelt thanks go to the many people who have helped make this book, especially Sam Elworthy, Sophia Broom and all at AUP, Reina Whaitiri for her blessing, Anna Hodge for saying go for it, Robert Sullivan for so beautifully curating the poems in te reo Māori, Elizabeth Caffin, David Eggleton, Anna Jackson and Gregory O'Brien for putting their respective and important oars in, Kiri Piahana-Wong for the most expert copy-editing, Sarah Ell for eagle-eyed proofreading, Floor van Lierop for stunning design, Rosalind Ali and Zech Soakai for their wonderful learning notes, Eileen Te Aho Kennedy for a truckload of typing, Temuera Sullivan for the inspiration of remembering poems, the amazing staff at Auckland City Libraries, especially Jane Wild at Central and staff at Mount Albert Library for not hiding when they saw me coming, and many friends for encouragement, including Serie Barford, David Brown, Mary Paul, Margaret Samuels and Michael Steven. My gratitude to Creative New Zealand for their funding towards this project. Last but not least, my deepest thanks to all the contributors who kindly allowed their poems to appear in this book, and whose superb work *is* this book. May their poems resound again and again into the airwaves!

Nō reira, tēnā koutou.

Recipient of a Prime Minister's Award for Literary Achievement, Anne Kennedy is the author of four novels, a novella, anthologised short stories and five collections of poetry. She is the two-time winner of the New Zealand Book Award for Poetry, for her collections *Sing-Song* and *The Darling North*. Her latest book of poetry, *The Sea Walks into the Wall,* was shortlisted for the 2022 Ockham New Zealand Book Awards.